1st EDITION

Perspectives on Diseases and Disorders

Lung Cancer

Jacqueline Langwith
Book Editor

PERSPECTIVES
On Diseases & Disorders

GALE
CENGAGE Learning™

Detroit • New York • San Francisco • New Haven, Conn • Waterville, Maine • London

Christine Nasso, *Publisher*
Elizabeth Des Chenes, *Managing Editor*

For more information, contact:
Greenhaven Press
27500 Drake Rd.
Farmington Hills, MI 48331-3535
Or you can visit our Internet site at gale.cengage.com

LIBRARY OF CONGRESS CATALOGING-IN-PUBLICATION DATA

Lung cancer / Jacqueline Langwith, book editor.
    p. cm. -- (Perspectives on diseases and disorders)
  Includes bibliographical references and index.
  ISBN 978-0-7377-5002-7 (hardcover)
  1. Lungs--Cancer. I. Langwith, Jacqueline.
  RC280.L8L76536 2011
  616.99'424--dc22

                                                                2010023163

Printed in the United States of America
  2 3 4 5 6 7 14 13 12 11

CONTENTS

FOREWORD

"Medicine, to produce health, has to examine disease."
—Plutarch

Independent research on a health issue is often the first step to complement discussions with a physician. But locating accurate, well-organized, understandable medical information can be a challenge. A simple Internet search on terms such as "cancer" or "diabetes," for example, returns an intimidating number of results. Sifting through the results can be daunting, particularly when some of the information is inconsistent or even contradictory. The Greenhaven Press series Perspectives on Diseases and Disorders offers a solution to the often overwhelming nature of researching diseases and disorders.

From the clinical to the personal, titles in the Perspectives on Diseases and Disorders series provide students and other researchers with authoritative, accessible information in unique anthologies that include basic information about the disease or disorder, controversial aspects of diagnosis and treatment, and first-person accounts of those impacted by the disease. The result is a well-rounded combination of primary and secondary sources that, together, provide the reader with a better understanding of the disease or disorder.

Each volume in Perspectives on Diseases and Disorders explores a particular disease or disorder in detail. Material for each volume is carefully selected from a wide range of sources, including encyclopedias, journals, newspapers, non-fiction books, speeches, government documents, pamphlets, organization newsletters, and position papers. Articles in the first chapter provide an authoritative, up-to-date overview that covers symptoms, causes and effects, treatments, cures, and medical advances. The second chapter presents a substantial number of opposing viewpoints on controversial treatments and other current debates relating to the volume topic. The third chapter offers a variety of personal perspectives on the disease or disorder. Patients, doctors, caregivers, and loved ones represent just some of the voices found in this narrative chapter.

Each Perspectives on Diseases and Disorders volume also includes:

- An **annotated table of contents** that provides a brief summary of each article in the volume.
- An **introduction** specific to the volume topic.
- Full-color **charts and graphs** to illustrate key points, concepts, and theories.
- Full-color **photos** that show aspects of the disease or disorder and enhance textual material.
- **"Fast Facts"** that highlight pertinent additional statistics and surprising points.
- A **glossary** providing users with definitions of important terms.
- A **chronology** of important dates relating to the disease or disorder.
- An annotated list of **organizations to contact** for students and other readers seeking additional information.
- A **bibliography** of additional books and periodicals for further research.
- A detailed **subject index** that allows readers to quickly find the information they need.

Whether a student researching a disorder, a patient recently diagnosed with a disease, or an individual who simply wants to learn more about a particular disease or disorder, a reader who turns to Perspectives on Diseases and Disorders will find a wealth of information in each volume that offers not only basic information, but also vigorous debate from multiple perspectives.

INTRODUCTION

In 2007 Australian Lisa Bowen documented her battle with stage IV lung cancer in the pages of her diary. She described moving from one cancer treatment to another as she tried to mount an effective battle against her lung cancer. She wrote of how scary it was to have to try a new treatment because it meant the previous treatment had been unsuccessful. More importantly, it also meant the cancer was getting stronger and her chances of recovery were getting dimmer. One of the treatments Bowen tried was Tarceva, a relatively new cancer drug first approved for use in 2004. Unfortunately, Tarceva did not work for Bowen, and she moved on to another cancer drug. However, Tarceva has been dramatically effective in beating back the lung cancer of other patients. Tarceva is one of a relatively new breed of lung cancer drugs that target specific genetic mutations.

Researchers discovered the concept of targeted cancer therapies almost by accident. Before drugs of any kind can be used by doctors to treat illness in the United States, they have to be approved by the U.S. Food and Drug Administration (FDA). Before the FDA will grant approval, a drug has to have been tested on hundreds of people in clinical trials to ensure that it is safe and effective. In clinical trials half of the group gets the drug, and the other half gets a placebo, or blank pill, that usually just contains sugar. Afterward, researchers look to see whether there is any statistical difference in the outcomes of the two groups. When researchers reviewed the overall results of the clinical trials for Tarceva and a similar drug called Iressa, the people who got the drugs seemed to do only marginally better than the people getting a placebo.

Statistically speaking, the results were not that striking, but were just good enough to get the drugs approved. It was when doctors actually started prescribing the drugs and observing the outcomes of individual patients—as opposed to looking at the overall statistical results of a large group of patients—that the true effectiveness of the drugs was revealed. As it turns out, the drugs did little if anything for some people, and Bowen fell into this group. However, there was another group of people who saw dramatic results.

What researchers found out was that people who respond to Tarceva and Iressa have a certain genetic mutation. In these people the gene that makes the epidermal growth factor receptor (EGFR) protein is mutated. EGFR proteins exist on the surface of mammalian cells, where they attract and bind to the epidermal growth factor protein. Researchers are not entirely sure why, but lung cancer patients with a mutated EGFR gene respond dramatically to Tarceva and Iressa. But for people like Bowen who do not have the mutation, the drugs are ineffective.

Targeted therapies are offering hope to many lung cancer patients. In the summer of 2009, Bill Schuette, a sixty-one-year-old Ohio man with stage IV lung cancer, watched a story on ABC's World News that changed his life. A short while before, Schuette had been told by his doctor that he had exhausted all his treatment options. He had already tried seven different cancer treatments, and Schuette realized his doctor was saying it was time "to go home and die." Schuette was devastated. However, after watching a story about targeted cancer therapies on World News, Schuette found renewed hope. He immediately enrolled in a clinical trial testing a new targeted therapy that was occurring at Massachusetts General Cancer Center.

Schuette was one of the lucky ones. Doctors analyzed a tumor from his lung and found that it contained a certain gene mutation that made it likely to respond to a new targeted therapy. The mutated gene in Schuette's tumor makes a protein called anaplastic lymphoma kinase, or ALK for short. The clinical trial Schuette enrolled in was testing whether a new drug made by Pfizer that targeted ALK mutations could help people with lung cancer. Schuette received the new drug—called crizotinib—and his cancer responded. He credits the World News story and crizotinib with saving his life. In a November 2009 story on the ABC News Web site, Schuette said that without the targeted treatment, "I would have died. There's no doubt in my mind. I mean, I was feeling bad. . . . The difference now is I'm alive and I feel good. . . . I have something to look forward to. Now I'm making plans again."[1]

Researchers from around the country are teaming up to look for new targeted lung cancer therapies. The Tumor Sequencing Project (TSP) is a collaboration of scientists from many prestigious research organizations, including Harvard, the Human Genome Sequencing Center at Baylor University, the M.D. Anderson Cancer Center at the University of Texas, and the University of Michigan Medical Center. The TSP group is examining approximately one thousand genes to look for mutations that may help researchers design other targeted therapies against lung cancers. In an April 2010 Reuters article, M.D. Anderson Cancer Center researcher Edwin Kim said, "We are still in the dark ages with how we treat lung cancer patients. Currently, they are separated only into histologic [tissue type] categories such as small cell or non-small cell lung cancer, with subtypes such as squamous or nonsquamous. As far as molecular testing nothing is typically done in lung cancer at this time."[2] Kim and other researchers would like to identify more genetic mutations associated with lung cancer tumors, develop customized therapies to target them, and screen everyone to determine their best treatment option. They have high expectations that someday there

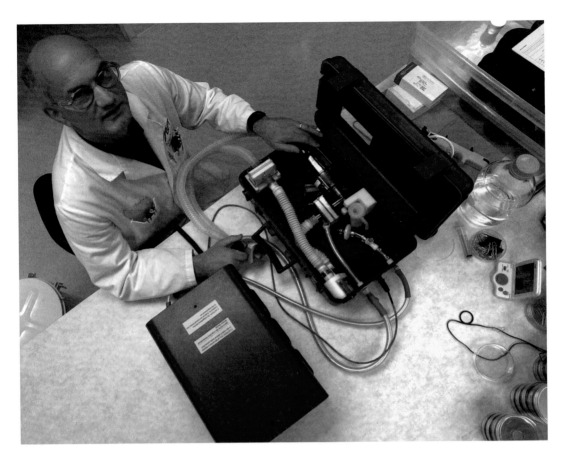

Among the many new ways to treat lung cancer is the use of an inhaler to administer drugs to patients. (AP Images)

will be a targeted therapy available to everyone who has lung cancer.

The hope offered by targeted therapies comes too late for Lisa Bowen. She succumbed to lung cancer a few months after trying Tarceva. Maybe Bowen's lung tumors had an as yet unidentified mutation that could have been targeted by a specific treatment. This thought—that people like Bowen could be saved by new treatments—drives lung cancer researchers to do all they can to defeat the number one cancer killer of men and women in the United States. In *Perspectives on Diseases and Disorders: Lung Cancer*, the contributors discuss other recent advances in lung cancer research, including research into the genetics of the disease. The authors also debate some of the controversial issues surrounding the causes, prevention, and diagnosis of lung cancer. Finally, the voices of people who have battled lung cancer—including Lisa Bowen—are also presented.

Notes

1. John McKenzie, "Experimental Drug Leads to Life Changing News for Cancer Patients," ABC News, November 10, 2009. http://abcnews.go.com/WN/cancer-patients-find-hope-experimental-drug-trials/story?id=9044249.
2. Deena Beasley, "Lung Cancer Drug Response Tied to Tumor Type-Study," Reuters, April 18, 2010. www.reuters.com/article/idUSN1614384620100418.

CHAPTER 1

Understanding Lung Cancer

An Overview of Lung Cancer

Cleveland Clinic

In the following viewpoint the Cleveland Clinic provides an overview of lung cancer. According to the clinic, there are two different types of lung cancer, small cell lung cancer and non-small cell lung cancer. The cancer cells of each type grow and spread in different ways and require different kinds of therapy. Of the two types, non-small cell lung cancer is the most common, and it is usually treated with surgery. Small cell lung cancer is harder to cure and is most commonly treated with chemotherapy. The authors say that lung cancer symptoms do not typically show up until the cancer is well established, and therefore early diagnosis is difficult. The Cleveland Clinic is a nonprofit academic medical center.

L ung cancer is a disease in which an abnormal, uncontrolled growth of cells occurs in the tissue of the lungs. The lungs are the breathing organs located in the chest. The lungs bring in fresh oxygen, which is distributed throughout the body by the blood. The lungs also remove carbon dioxide, a waste product, from the blood.

SOURCE: Cleveland Clinic, "Lung Cancer Overview," October 23, 2008. Reproduced by permission.

Photo on facing page. Gene therapy involves viral delivery of new genes to replace defective ones. Areas of the body treated include the brain, heart, lungs, pancreas, and colon. **(Laguna Design/Photo Researchers, Inc.)**

The lungs are spongy organs that are surrounded by a thin, protective membrane called the pleura. Each lung is divided into lobes; the right lung has three lobes, and the left lung has two lobes. Within the lungs are flexible airways called bronchi, which branch out into many smaller airways called bronchioles. The bronchioles lead to small, grape-like clusters of air sacs called alveoli. Oxygen and carbon dioxide pass to and from the alveoli into capillaries, the smallest of the vessels that carry blood throughout the body.

Lung cancer develops when a cell in the lung becomes abnormal and begins to duplicate uncontrollably. These abnormal cells eventually form a mass, or tumor, and can spread to other parts of the body if not treated. This spreading of cancer cells is called metastasis.

There are two major types of lung cancer: small cell lung cancer and non-small cell lung cancer. The cancer cells of each type grow and spread in different ways, and they are treated differently.

Small Cell Lung Cancer

Small cell lung cancer accounts for about 15% of all lung cancers. As the name implies, small cell lung cancer involves cancer cells that are smaller in size than most other cancer cells. Although the cells are small, they are able to quickly reproduce and form large tumors, as well as to spread to other parts of the body. There are two stages of small cell lung cancer:

- Limited refers to cancer that is confined to the chest.
- Extensive refers to lung cancer that has spread to other areas beyond the chest.

The rapidly dividing small cell lung cancers do respond to chemotherapy (drug therapy that attacks growing, dividing cells) but are difficult to cure. In general, limited small cell lung cancer is treated with chemotherapy and radiation therapy. Extensive small cell lung cancer most often is treated solely with chemotherapy.

Non-small Cell Lung Cancer

Non-small cell lung cancer is the most common form of lung cancer, accounting for about 85% of all lung cancers. As you might expect, the cells of non-small lung cancer are larger than those of small cell lung cancer. There are several different types of non-small cell lung cancers, based on the type of cells found in the cancer. The most common types of non-small cell lung cancer include:

- Squamous cell carcinoma (also called epidermoid carcinoma) begins in the special cells, called epithelial cells, which line the air passages. Thus it may occur within the larger breathing tubes. If not treated, this cancer may spread to the lymph nodes, bones, adrenal gland, liver, and brain. It is a common cancer, making up approximately 25% of all lung cancers in the United States. The most common cause of squamous cell carcinoma is smoking.
- Adenocarcinoma usually begins in the mucus-producing cells of the lungs. It is the most common type of lung cancer in the United States. While it has been linked to smoking, adenocarcinoma is the most common type of lung cancer in non-smokers. In most cases, adenocarcinoma develops slowly. In other cases, the cancer develops more quickly and can be rapidly fatal. When it spreads, it often spreads to the brain. Other common sites for metastasis include the other lung, lymph nodes, the liver, the adrenal glands and bone.
- Large cell carcinoma is responsible for about 10% to 20% of lung cancers. Large cell carcinomas include all lung cancers that cannot be classified as squamous cell carcinomas or adenocarcinomas.

Non-small cell cancer usually is treated by surgery, taking out the cancer in an operation, if it is diagnosed at an early stage, before it has spread to any other area in the body. Chemotherapy and radiation therapy are other treatment options. These are used when the cancer has spread to areas of the body beyond the primary tumor, or when the person with lung cancer is not healthy enough to tolerate surgery. At times they are used with the intention of curing the cancer. When the cancer has spread too far to cure, they can be very effective at improving the quality of life and extending survival.

Symptoms and Causes

Lung cancer often produces no symptoms until the disease is well established and/or has spread to other parts of the body. When symptoms do appear, they may include:

- Frequent bouts of bronchitis (inflammation and swelling of the bronchi) or pneumonia (an infection that occurs when fluid collects in the lungs)
- Coughing, especially coughing up blood
- Wheezing
- Weight loss or loss of appetite
- Hoarseness
- Swelling of the face or arms
- Fever
- Shortness of breath
- Pain in the shoulders, chest or back

Smoking (cigarettes, pipes or cigars) is the cause of 85% of all cases of lung cancer. Cigarette smoke contains more than 4,000 chemicals, many of which are proven to cause cancer. Research suggests that the chemicals formed when tobacco is burned, inhaled and absorbed by the lungs trigger a change in the cells, which leads to cancer. Tobacco smoke also contains harmful gases, such as nitrogen oxide and carbon monoxide.

Other risk factors for lung cancer also have been identified. Risk factors for lung cancer include:

- Exposure to radon—Radon is an odorless, colorless gas that is produced naturally from the breakdown of uranium. Radon often is present in soil and wa-

Basic Information About Lung Cancer

Lung cancers are cancers that begin in the lungs. Other types of cancers may spread to the lungs from other organs. However, these are not lung cancers because they did not start in the lungs. When cancer cells spread from one organ to another, they are called "metastases."

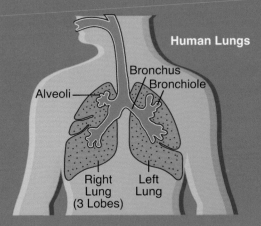

Human Lungs

Bronchus
Bronchiole
Alveoli
Right Lung (3 Lobes)
Left Lung

Research has found several risk factors for lung cancer. A risk factor is anything that changes the risk of getting a disease. Different risk factors change risk by different amounts.

The risk factors for lung cancer include:
Smoking and being around others' smoke
Things around us at home or work (such as radon gas)
Personal traits (such as having a family history of lung cancer)

Taken from: Division of Cancer Prevention and Control, National Center for Chronic Disease Prevention and Health Promotion, Centers for Disease Control and Prevention.

ter, and can get into the air we breathe. High levels of radon can occur in certain work environments and in homes, where it can seep in undetected.
• Exposure to chemicals—Workers exposed to certain chemicals have a higher risk for lung cancer.

These chemicals include asbestos, nickel, mustard gas, and silica.

- Family history—Having a family history of the disease also may increase the risk of developing lung cancer.
- History of lung disease—People with other lung diseases, such as COPD [chronic obstructive pulmonary disease] or pulmonary fibrosis, are at an increased risk of developing lung cancer.
- Second-hand smoke—Exposure to smoke from others' cigarettes can increase the risk of developing lung cancer.
- Diet—Diets low in fruits, vegetables and grains may increase the risk of lung cancer.
- Marijuana use—Studies have shown that long-term smoking of marijuana can cause cancer of the airways (bronchial tubes) leading to the lungs.

Smoking is the cause of 85 percent of all lung cancer cases. (© 24BY36/Alamy)

According to the American Cancer Society, more than 200,000 Americans are diagnosed with lung cancer each year. It is the number one cause of cancer death for both men and women in the United States. Overall, Americans have about a 7% chance of developing lung cancer during their lifetimes.

Lung cancer usually occurs in people over 50 years old who have a long history of cigarette smoking. Overall, lung cancer is more common in men than in women, although adenocarcinoma—a form of non-small cell lung cancer—is more common in women. Lung cancer also affects African Americans more often than Caucasians.

Diagnosis and Treatment

Because early lung cancer often has no symptoms, it is difficult to diagnose the disease in its early stages. Some diagnostic tests that may be used include:

- Sputum test—Your phlegm, or spit, is studied to see if cancer cells from the lungs are present.
- Chest X-ray—X-rays use low doses of radiation to create images of the body.
- Computed tomography (CT or CAT) scan—This is a special X-ray that uses a computer to create a series of images, or slices, of the inside of the body.
- Magnetic resonance imaging (MRI) scan—This is a test that produces images of the inside of the body using a large magnet, radio waves and a computer.
- Positron emission tomography (PET) scan—This is a technique to obtain three-dimensional, color images using short-lived radioactive substances. Unlike X-rays and CT scans, which provide images of the structures in the body, PET scans help the doctor evaluate body function. The PET scan can detect cancerous tumors because of their ability to absorb the radioactive material.

- Bronchoscopy—During this test, the doctor looks into the bronchi through a special instrument, called a bronchoscope, that slides down the throat and into the bronchial tubes. The lighted end of the tube allows the doctor to see any abnormal areas. If abnormal tissue is found, the doctor can take cells from the walls of the bronchial tubes or cut small pieces of tissue to look at under the microscope to see if there are any cancer cells. This is called a biopsy.
- Needle aspiration biopsy—The doctor also may use a needle to remove tissue from a place in the lung that may be hard to reach with the bronchoscope. The needle will be put through the skin, in between the ribs, under the guidance of a CT scan. This is called a needle aspiration biopsy. The doctor will look at the tissue under the microscope to see if there are any cancer cells.
- Mediastinoscopy—This is a procedure in which the doctor inserts a lighted tube through a small incision (cut) above the breast bone to view the structures of the center of the chest. (The mediastinum is the space inside the central part of the chest, between the lungs.)
- Surgical lung biopsy—The doctor also may look inside your chest cavity with a special instrument called a thoracoscope. To do this surgical procedure—called a thoracoscopy—the doctor makes several small cuts in the chest wall, and inserts the thoracoscope and other instruments into the chest between the ribs. The doctor can examine the chest cavity and take tissue samples (biopsies) from the lungs. Standard surgical sampling of the lung may also be required.

Once lung cancer has been found (diagnosis), tests will be done to find out if the cancer has spread from the lung to other parts of the body (staging). A doctor needs to know the stage to plan treatment. Some of the tests that may be used to stage the disease are the aforementioned CT, PET, and MRI scans as well as non-surgical and surgical biopsies.

Treatment of lung cancer depends on the type of cancer, the stage of the disease, and the patient's age and overall condition. Treatments used include:

- Radiation therapy uses X-rays or other high-energy rays to kill cancer cells and shrink tumors. Radiation may come from a machine outside the body (external radiation therapy) or from putting materials that produce radiation (radioisotopes) through thin plastic tubes in the area where the cancer cells are found (internal radiation therapy). Radiation therapy can be used alone or in addition to surgery and/or chemotherapy.

- Chemotherapy uses drugs to kill cancer cells. Chemotherapy may be taken by pill, or it may be put into the body by a needle in the vein or muscle. Chemotherapy is called a systemic treatment because the drug enters the bloodstream, travels through the body, and can kill cancer cells outside the lungs.

- Surgery—Non-small cell cancer may be treated by surgery if it is found early enough in an otherwise healthy person. There are four basic operations used to treat non-small cell lung cancer.

- Sleeve resection is a procedure that removes the cancerous portion of the airway, but leaves enough healthy tissue to reconnect the edges of the bronchi, thus preserving function.

- Limited, or wedge, resection is an operation that takes out a segment, or wedge, of the lung to remove the area with the cancer.

> **FAST FACT**
>
> According to the National Cancer Institute, there were 159,390 deaths from lung cancer in the United States in 2009.

- Lobectomy is the removal of a section (lobe) of the lung.
- Pneumonectomy is the removal of an entire lung.
- Clinical trials—A clinical trial is a research program conducted with patients to evaluate a new medical treatment, drug or device. Clinical trials are ongoing in most parts of the country for all stages of lung cancer.

The prognosis (chance of recovery) and choice of treatment depend on the stage of the cancer (whether it is just in the lung or has spread to other places), tumor size, the type of lung cancer, whether there are symptoms, and the patient's general health. Early detection is critical to improving the chances of treatment success and survival. Unfortunately, there are no currently approved screening tests for lung cancer.

Not smoking is the best way to prevent lung cancer. Eating a healthy diet, avoiding second-hand smoke, and taking precautions when working around asbestos and other chemicals also may help you reduce your risk.

Genes May Predispose Some People to Lung Cancer

Seth Borenstein

In the following viewpoint Seth Borenstein discusses a scientific discovery that has pinpointed genes that make people more susceptible to cigarette addiction and more prone to lung cancer. According to the article, a smoker who inherits these genetic variants from both parents has a much greater chance of lung cancer than a smoker without the genetic variants. It is still unclear whether the variants directly or indirectly—by causing smoking—increase lung cancer risk. Borenstein is a regular reporter for Associated Press Online.

Scientists have pinpointed genetic variations that make people more likely to get hooked on cigarettes and more prone to develop lung cancer—a finding that could someday lead to screening tests and customized treatments for smokers trying to kick the habit.

The discovery by three separate teams of scientists makes the strongest case so far for the biological underpinnings of nicotine addiction and sheds more light on how genetics and lifestyle habits join forces to cause cancer.

SOURCE: Seth Borenstein, "Smoking Habit, Lung Cancer in the Genes," AP Online, April 2, 2008. Reproduced by permission.

"This is kind of a double whammy gene," said Christopher Amos, a professor of epidemiology at the M.D. Anderson Cancer Center in Houston and author of one of the studies. "It also makes you more likely to be dependent on smoking and less likely to quit smoking."

The Genes of It All

A smoker who inherits these genetic variations from both parents has an 80 percent greater chance of lung cancer than a smoker without the variants, the researchers reported. And that same smoker on average lights up two extra cigarettes a day and has a much harder time quitting than smokers who don't have these genetic differences.

The researchers disagreed on whether the variants directly increased the risk of lung cancer or did so indirectly, by causing more smoking.

The three studies, funded by governments in the U.S. and Europe, is being published Thursday [April 3, 2008] in the journals *Nature* and *Nature Genetics*.

The scientists studied the genes of more than 35,000 people in Europe, Canada and the United States. They aren't quite sure if what they found is a set of variations in one gene or in three closely connected genes.

The gene variations, which govern nicotine receptors on cells, could eventually help explain some of the mysteries of chain smoking, nicotine addiction and lung cancer. These oddities include why there are 90-year-old smokers who don't get cancer and people who light up an occasional cigarette and don't get hooked.

"This is really telling us that the vulnerability to smoking and how much you smoke is clearly biologically based," said psychiatry professor Dr. Laura Bierut of Washington University in St. Louis, a genetics and smoking expert who did not take part in the studies. She praised the research as "very intriguing."

The Surprise of the Genetics

The smoking rate among U.S. adults has dropped from 42 percent in 1965 to less than 21 percent now.

The new studies are surprising in that they point to areas of the genetic code that are not associated with pleasure and the rewards of addiction.

That may help explain why some people can quit and others fail, said Dr. Nora Volkow, director of the National Institute of Drug Abuse in Bethesda, Md., which funded one of the studies.

"It opens our eyes," Volkow said Wednesday. "Not everyone takes drugs for the same reason. Not everyone smokes cigarettes for the same reasons."

One clue is in the location of the just-discovered variants, on the long arm of chromosome 15, Volkow said. It is in an area that, when damaged during tests on animals, makes them depressed and anxious. While some people smoke because it helps them focus or gives them a physiological reward, others do it to stave off depression.

That suggests that adding antidepressants to some smokers' treatment could help them kick the habit.

Bierut said a simple, inexpensive test could be developed to screen people for the variants. Kari Stefansson, lead author of the largest of the three studies, agreed. He is chief executive of deCode Genetics of Iceland, which already does prostate cancer genetic tests.

Such testing could carry risks all its own, bioethicist Arthur Caplan of the University of Pennsylvania warned. People who have been found to have a genetic predisposition to addiction and lung cancer could find it harder to get health or life insurance, or their employer might drop their coverage, he said.

"The good news is that getting these risk estimates will help focus anti-smoking campaigns, and some people

> **FAST FACT**
>
> More people die from lung cancer than any other cancer, according to the Centers for Disease Control and Prevention.

will want to voluntarily get into anti-addiction programs early, where they will probably work better," Caplan said in an e-mail. But if such testing is done, it should be voluntary, and the results should be kept private, he said.

The research involved only white people of European descent. Blacks and Asians will be studied soon and may yield quite different results, scientists said.

Smoking-related diseases worldwide kill about one in 10 adults, according to the World Health Organization.

Among the Findings:

- Smokers who get the set of variants from only one parent see a risk of lung cancer that is about one-third higher than that of people without the variants. They also smoke about one more cigarette a day on average than other smokers. This group makes up about 45 percent of the population studied.
- Smokers who inherit the variants from both parents have nearly a 1-in-4 chance of developing lung cancer. Their cancer risk is 70 to 80 percent higher than that of smokers without the genetic variants. They smoke on average two extra cigarettes a day. This group accounts for about one in nine people of European descent.
- Smokers who don't have the variants are still more than 10 times more likely to get lung cancer than nonsmokers. Smokers without the variant have about a 14 percent risk of getting lung cancer. The risk of lung cancer for people who have never smoked is less than 1 percent, said another study author, Paul Brennan of the International Agency for Research on Cancer in Lyon, France.

Brennan and Amos, working on different teams, linked the genetic variation itself—when triggered by smoking—directly to lung cancer. Brennan said the nicotine receptors that the variants act on also can stimulate tumor growth.

Studies suggest that the tendency to smoke, as well as how much one smokes, may be genetically based. Smoking cessation drugs, such as those available in gum form (foreground), can aid in quitting the habit. (**Steve Percival/ Photo Researchers, Inc.**)

But Stefansson said the increased lung cancer risk was indirect—the variants led to more smoking, which led to more cancer.

For Stefansson, the research hits home. His father, a smoker, died of lung cancer. And Stefansson, who doesn't smoke, frequently lectures his 23-year-old daughter "who smokes like a chimney." She acts as if she is immortal and smoking can't kill her, Stefansson said. But his own research shows that her genes are probably stacked against her.

Genes May Be Key in Helping to Fight Lung Cancer

Maggie Fox

In the following viewpoint Maggie Fox reports that a person's genetic profile may help doctors target lung cancer treatments. Fox says that lung cancer treatments are generally hit-or-miss, in that some patients are helped while others are not. However, studies seem to indicate that lung cancer treatments can be designed on the basis of the different genes people carry. For instance, researchers have found that the genes associated with lung cancer in men are different than they are in women. This means that the prognosis and treatment of lung cancer in women and men are different. Fox is the health and science editor for Reuters news service.

Lung cancer is often dramatically different in women than it is in men, U.S. researchers reported on Tuesday [February 9, 2010] in another study that suggests ways to tailor treatment for cancer patients.

SOURCE: Maggie Fox, "Researchers Find Sex-Specific Lung Cancer Genes," Yahoo! News, February 9, 2010. Reproduced by permission of Thomson Reuters.

They also found that some elderly patients have forms of lung cancer that make them likely to benefit from chemotherapy, even though the treatments can be harsh.

The study, published in the *Journal of the American Medical Association*, is the latest in a string of experiments that show cancer is far more complex genetically than doctors dreamed of even a few years ago.

Together, the studies may open better ways to target the hit-and-miss treatments that can sicken some patients while saving the lives of others.

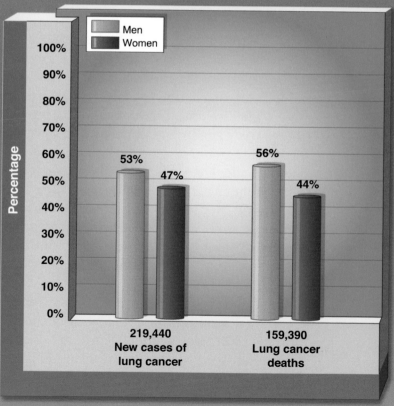

Lung Cancer in Men and Women in the United States, 2009

Taken from: National Cancer Institute, National Institutes of Health.

Dr. Anil Potti of Duke University in North Carolina and colleagues studied 787 patients with non-small cell lung cancer, looking at how well they did on treatment and analyzing their DNA.

They looked at genes known to be involved in cancer....

"Our study supports two key findings: First, the biology of lung cancer in women is dramatically different from what we see in men," Potti said in a statement.

"Women, in general, have a less complex disease, at least in terms of the numbers of molecular pathways involved. We also discovered that there is a subset of elderly patients [who] would probably benefit from treatments that we've normally reserved for younger patients."

Some of the findings were not surprising. Patients whose cancer came back the quickest after treatment had tumors rich in genes activated for tumor spread or those that help tumors grow new blood supplies.

FAST FACT

Overall, the chance that a man will develop lung cancer in his lifetime is about one in thirteen; for a woman the risk is about one in sixteen, according to the American Cancer Society.

Thousands of Mutations

The researchers noted that genetic cancer tests are far more available than in the past and often deliver results within a week. It may be possible to start defining patients by their specific genetic tumor signatures, they said.

In December [2009] British scientists who sequenced all the DNA from lung tumor tissue said they found more than 23,000 mutations.

Several cancer drugs are already targeted to some of the genetic mutations the researchers found, and studies have hinted at some of the variability seen in lung cancer....

Lung cancer is the leading cause of cancer death globally, killing 1.3 million people a year. It does not cause symptoms right away so most people are diagnosed after it has spread—one reason the survival rate is only about 15 percent.

A researcher examines the genetic sequence of a segment of cancer DNA. Studies seem to indicate that lung cancer treatments can be designed on the basis of a person's genetic makeup. (Colin Cuthbert/Photo Researchers, Inc.)

There are dozens of drugs on the market to treat lung cancer and oncologists make an art of matching the therapy to the patient.

"So being able to better understand the disease and stratify patients by their individual molecular profiles means we can do a much better job pairing the right drug with the right patient," said Duke's Dr. Jeffrey Crawford, who worked on the study.

A New Lung Cancer Treatment Approach Raises Hopes and Debate

Carmen Phillips

In the following viewpoint Carmen Phillips discusses a new approach to cancer treatment, called maintenance therapy, which may prolong the lives of people with certain types of lung cancer. Maintenance therapy consists of several cycles of chemotherapy treatments given immediately in a row, without the typical resting period in between. According to Phillips, clinical trials indicate that people with non-small cell lung cancer of the nonsquamous type saw improvements when they received maintenance therapy. Many doctors are hopeful that maintenance therapy can prolong the lives of some lung cancer patients. However, says Phillips, other doctors are skeptical of the benefits of the therapy. Phillips is an award-winning writer for the *NCI Cancer Bulletin*, an online newsletter published by the National Cancer Institute.

A number of clinical trials have tried and failed to improve survival in patients who have advanced non-small cell lung cancer (NSCLC) by extending the duration of their initial treatment. The premise behind the approach, often called maintenance therapy,

SOURCE: Carmen Phillips, "New Lung Cancer Approach Raises Hopes and Debate," *NCI Cancer Bulletin*, July 28, 2009.

is simple: In patients whose tumors regress following their initial treatment, give the cancer another kick while it's down, rather than waiting for it to regain steam before delivering further therapy.

Where past trials have failed, though, several recent phase III trials using more current agents have reported some success using maintenance therapy. To date, one trial has reported improved overall survival and a second, the SATURN trial, is slated to report improved overall survival next week [August 2009] at an international lung cancer conference. Several other trials have shown improvements in progression-free survival. Among patients with advanced disease, for whom survival can range from a few months to 1 or 2 years, any improvement is good news. . . .

Scientists Debate the Role of Maintenance Therapy

Even with the positive data, though, leading lung cancer experts disagree on some important details about precisely how maintenance therapy fits into the current treatment mix for advanced NSCLC, which now includes numerous options for first-, second-, and third-line treatments, some of which are targeted therapies.

The debate over maintenance chemotherapy has taken on renewed importance in recent weeks, with the FDA's [Food and Drug Administration] approval of the first agent for use in this indication, pemetrexed (Alimta). Just how deeply this new treatment approach will reach into the clinic is unclear. According to Dr. Sherman Baker, Jr., of Virginia Commonwealth University's Massey Cancer Center, it's already being done on a limited basis and its use is now likely to expand.

"The question in my mind is, will we do it right?" he said. That is, will clinicians follow the approaches that clinical trials have shown offer a benefit? Dr. Baker also wonders if these trials will alter cancer specialists' mindset.

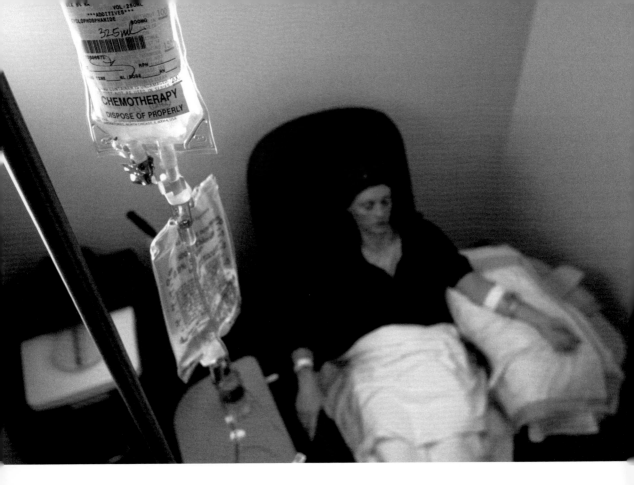

Maintenance therapy involves administering several cycles of chemotherapy treatments, without the customary resting period between cycles. (Sam Ogden/Photo Researchers, Inc.)

"Will these trials change how we view advanced NSCLC—not just as a disease that is always fatal but as something that we may be able to make more of a chronic disease, where 2-year survivals are more common?"

Although there is some disagreement on the role of maintenance therapy, there is no question about the duration of first-line chemotherapy in patients with advanced NSCLC—four to six cycles (most often four)—or that first-line chemotherapy should consist of a combination of agents that include a platinum chemotherapy drug such as cisplatin or carboplatin. Numerous trials have shown that these platinum-based "doublets" are highly effective, but that going beyond six cycles simply piles on toxicity without any added clinical benefit.

PERSPECTIVES ON DISEASES AND DISORDERS

Maintenance therapy—as practiced in the phase III clinical trials that have reported positive results—comes into play in patients whose tumors have responded to first-line therapy. These patients then immediately begin treatment with maintenance agents until their disease shows signs of progressing.

In the international phase III trial that garnered pemetrexed's FDA approval for this new indication, patients with advanced NSCLC of the nonsquamous type had a median overall survival of 15.5 months with pemetrexed

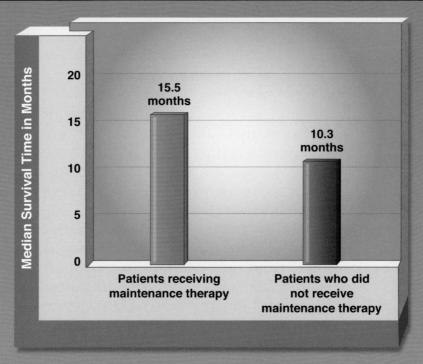

Maintenance Therapy Prolongs Survival Time

In patients with advanced non-small cell lung cancer of the nonsquamous type:

Median Survival Time in Months

- 20
- 15.5 months
- 15
- 10.3 months
- 10
- 5
- 0

Patients receiving maintenance therapy

Patients who did not receive maintenance therapy

Taken from: Carmen Phillips, "New Lung Cancer Treatment Approach Raises Hopes and Debate," *NCI Cancer Bulletin*, July 28, 2009.

maintenance therapy, compared with 10.3 months for those who received best supportive care. Progression-free survival also improved significantly. Patients with squamous cell carcinoma [a certain type of non-small cell lung cancer] did not benefit from the maintenance therapy regimen.

Dr. Chandra P. Belani, the trial's principal investigator, believes the trial results establish maintenance therapy as a new standard of care for nonsquamous NSCLC. "Such a survival benefit with maintenance therapy has not been seen before," he said. Given the low rate of less-severe side effects seen with pemetrexed, he added, the potential survival benefits warrant its use.

FAST FACT

Nearly a quarter of all new cases of lung cancer are small cell lung cancer, and most of these patients die in the first year after diagnosis, according to the Cochrane Collaboration.

"Whenever there is something new, there are going to be those who are reluctant to use it," Dr. Belani said. "But now that it is approved [by the FDA] based on the trial results, how can you deny it to patients?"

Dr. Nasser Hanna, from Indiana University's Simon Cancer Center, remains skeptical of maintenance chemotherapy for most patients with advanced NSCLC. The survival benefit in the pemetrexed trial, he argued, is not quite what it seems because many patients in the trial's non-maintenance arm did not receive the study drug or any approved second-line therapy once their disease progressed. And even low-grade toxicities, he added, "are not trivial," particularly in this patient population.

Similar results, Dr. Hanna continued, can be achieved in many patients even if they get a "holiday" from treatment—referring to the practice of giving patients time to recover from the duress of first-line treatment—or even if, as current guidelines recommend, the next round of treatment is not initiated until there are signs of progression.

In another positive maintenance therapy trial that used the chemotherapy drug docetaxel (Taxotere), published earlier this year [2009], a significant percentage of patients in the non-maintenance arm did not receive docetaxel upon disease progression. However, patients who did had the same survival as those who received it immediately.

"I don't see these trials as demonstrating that maintenance therapy is necessary for the majority of patients," Dr. Hanna said. "But they do underscore the value of these agents in metastatic [spreading] disease and the importance of not losing the opportunity to treat patients with these drugs."

That limited window of opportunity, argued Dr. Belani, is exactly why immediate administration of therapy is so important. "There is no way to predict which patient will benefit from a treatment holiday," he said. "After a treatment holiday, a third of patients can't go on to [receive the next] treatment. They either have a declining performance status, their cancer progresses, or they die."

Do Not Ignore Symptoms

A key point to take away from the recent positive maintenance therapy trials is that they all involved FDA-approved second- and third-line treatments, said Dr. Mark Socinski from the University of North Carolina's Lineberger Comprehensive Cancer Center. This is a big change from earlier in this decade, he noted, when there were fewer effective first-line therapies for NSCLC, let alone anything beyond that.

"These trials are telling us that it's important for patients to get drugs known to improve survival," he said. "A maintenance strategy is one way to do that." Regardless of the strategy that's chosen, Dr. Socinski continued, the available data indicate that oncologists need to more closely consider the next line of therapy and educate their patients about it.

"We need to tell them, if your cough gets worse, if the pain gets worse, don't wait for your next appointment. Don't ignore your symptoms," he said. "Patients need to hear that something like that means their disease might be getting worse, and they need to know that getting active agents can help."

Tobacco Smoke Causes Inflammation and Promotes Tumor Growth

NewsRx Health

In the following viewpoint NewsRx Health reports on research that indicates that tobacco smoke can make lung cancer worse. The article contends that it has been well-known that tobacco smoke can cause cancer-inducing mutations, but after a study by Michael Karin, it was found that exposure to smoke enhanced tumor formation and lung inflammation. NewsRx Health is the world's largest source of health information.

Repeated exposure to tobacco smoke makes lung cancer much worse, and one reason is that it steps up inflammation in the lung. Scientists at the University of California, San Diego School of Medicine have found that mice with early lung cancer lesions that were repeatedly exposed to tobacco smoke developed larger tumors—and developed tumors more quickly—than unexposed animals. The key contributing factor was lung tissue inflammation.

SOURCE: NewsRx Health, "Tobacco Smoke Causes Lung Inflammation, Promotes Lung Cancer Growth," February 7, 2010. Reproduced by permission.

The results of their study, published January 19 [2010] in the journal *Cancer Cell*, provide definitive evidence for the role of lung inflammation brought on by chronic exposure to tobacco smoke in promoting lung cancer growth. The findings also establish new lung cancer models, provide insights into both the development and growth of lung cancer, and suggest the possibility of using anti-inflammatory agents to prevent or slow lung cancer progression, said Michael Karin, PhD, Distinguished Professor of Pharmacology and Pathology at the UC San Diego School of Medicine, who led the work.

Promoting Tumors and Inflammation

"We've shown for the first time that tobacco smoke is a tumor promoter—not only a tumor initiator—and that it works through inflammation," said Karin, director of the Laboratory of Gene Regulation and Signal Transduction and a member of the Moores UCSD Cancer Center. "Other particulate materials, such as fine silicon dust, asbestos and coal dust, may promote lung cancer development through similar mechanisms.

Such substances were never found to induce mutations, which are the essence of tumor formation. More research is needed to explore the role and biochemical mechanisms of exposure to pro-inflammatory substances in the environment in early stages of cancer development."

Lung cancer killed nearly 160,000 Americans in 2009, according to the American Cancer Society, making it the leading cause of cancer death in both men and women.

It's well known that tobacco smoke can cause cancer-inducing mutations and other types of lung disease, as well as pulmonary inflammation. Karin's team wanted to know whether tobacco smoke could actively promote tumor growth once the cancerous process began and, if so, whether the tumor-promoting ability of tobacco smoke was due to inflammation.

FAST FACT

Kentucky has the highest rate of lung cancer among the states, according to the Centers for Disease Control and Prevention.

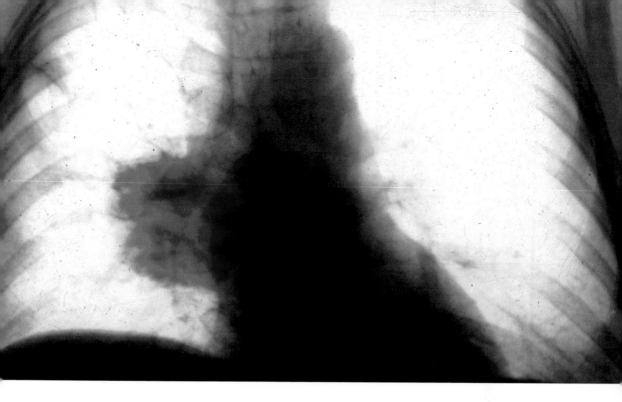

A digitally-enhanced chest X-ray shows a large cancerous lesion in red. (Scott Camazine/ Photo Reseachers, Inc.)

Karin and his group initiated lung tumors in mice, either by giving them a chemical carcinogen or by introducing a mutated gene, KRAS, into their genome. The mice were then intermittently exposed to tobacco smoke. The researchers found that exposure to smoke enhanced tumor formation, causing larger tumors that grew more quickly than those in mice that were not exposed.

Smoke-Inflammation Relationship

To determine a smoke-inflammation relationship, they inactivated nuclear factor kappa B (NF-κB)—a transcription factor known to be a common link between inflammation and cancer—in immune cells called macrophages and neutrophils, and found that this inhibited smoke-promoted tumor development in both chemically and genetically induced lung cancers in mice. Inactivation of NF-κB in macrophages and neutrophils also prevented smoke-induced lung inflammation.

Short-term tobacco smoke exposure in mice may turn on certain biochemical signals—a pair of "signaling

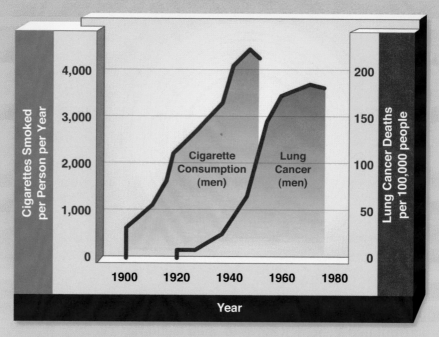

Twenty-Year Lag Time Between Smoking and Lung Cancer

Taken from: National Institutes of Health.

pathways" called IKK and JNK. This, in turn, ramps up the production of inflammatory substances, promoting tumor growth, Karin said. In addition to providing a more complete explanation for the cancer-causing ability of tobacco smoke, this work suggests new avenues for lung cancer prevention and treatment.

"If scientists can look in lung cancer tumor tissue samples and see that inflammation markers—such as NF-κB, IL-6 and TNF, which we found in mice—are also present in human lung cancer, we can then build a strong case for the use of anti-inflammatory drugs to treat patients who have been diagnosed in the early stage of lung cancer," said contributor David H. Broide, MD, UCSD Professor of Medicine.

Lung Cancer Is Different in Nonsmokers

Charles M. Rudin, Erika Avila-Tang, and Jonathan M. Sarnet

In the following viewpoint Charles M. Rudin, Erika Avila-Tang, and Jonathan M. Sarnet discuss the differences in lung cancer between smokers and nonsmokers. According to the authors, lung cancer affects significant numbers of people who have never smoked a day in their lives. The authors say that the cancerous tumors found in never smokers are significantly different from the tumors found in smokers. The treatment and prognosis of lung cancer in never smokers are different as well. The authors say that more research into lung cancer in never smokers is needed. Rudin is a professor in the Oncology Department at the Johns Hopkins Medical School; Sarnet is the director of the Johns Hopkins Institute for Global Tobacco Control; and Avila-Tang is an epidemiologist at the institute.

SOURCE: Charles M. Rudin, Erika Avila-Tang, and Jonathan M. Sarnet, "Lung Cancer in Never Smokers: A Call to Action," *Clinical Cancer Research*, September 2009, pp. 5622–624.

L̲ung cancer caused by tobacco smoking is a well-documented public health tragedy. This highly fatal and largely avoidable cancer now causes more than 1 million deaths worldwide each year and more than 160,000 deaths annually in the United States. Lung cancer is responsible for more American deaths than colon cancer, breast cancer, and prostate cancer combined. An estimated 90% of cases are linked to cigarette smoking, based on the American Cancer Society's Cancer Prevention Study II.

The exceptionally high risk for lung cancer in smokers has obscured the problem of lung cancer in never smokers. Not all cases of lung cancer can be attributed to current or former smoking, and several environmental risk factors for lung cancer other than smoking have been identified. Worldwide, clear estimates of the number of lung cancer cases in never smokers are not consistently available, but several populations have been described with particularly high rates that are not readily explained. In the United States, lung cancer in never smokers is almost as common a cause of death as atherosclerosis [hardening of the arteries] and is among the most common causes of cancer mortality. . . .

What Is Known About Lung Cancer in People Who Never Smoked

- Lung cancer in never smokers is a worldwide public health concern, with incidence and mortality similar to many other major cancer types. In the United States, it is as common a cause of death as cancer of the liver or of the esophagus.
- Some causal risk factors for lung cancer in never smokers have been identified. These include second-hand exposure to tobacco smoke, radon and other ionizing radiation, asbestos, indoor air pollution, underlying chronic lung disease, and family history.

Common Types of Cancer Deaths in the United States, 2008

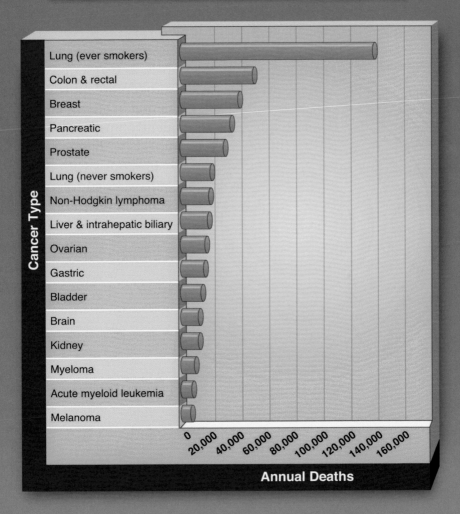

Taken from: Charles M. Rudin, Erika Avila-Tang, and Jonathan M. Samet, "Lung Cancer in Never Smokers: A Call to Action," *Clinical Cancer Research*, September 15, 2009.

• Estimates for the United States indicate that about half of cases are attributable to indoor radon in homes or to exposure to second-hand smoke. However, the relative importance of the various risk factors in contributing to disease burden worldwide is not clearly defined and likely varies from country to country. In some places, indoor exposure to smoke from biomass fuel combustion is a major contributor.

- Overall, comparing lung cancers in never smokers and ever smokers, there are clinically significant differences in tumor biology, prognosis, and response to therapy. Tumors arising in never smokers are more often adenocarcinomas [cancer originating in glands and other epithelial tissue] and infrequently small cell or squamous cell carcinomas. Never smokers with lung cancer have a better natural history and prognosis with therapy than ever smokers with lung cancer. In comparison to lung cancers in smokers, cancers in never smokers are more

Several risk factors for lung cancer in nonsmokers have been identified, including exposure to tobacco smoke, family history, and asbestos. (Philippe Garo/Photo Researchers, Inc.)

likely to have EGFR mutations [errors in the gene that makes epidermal growth factor receptors] and to benefit from treatment with epidermal growth factor receptor (EGFR) . . . inhibitors.

- Research on lung cancer in never smokers may improve understanding of lung cancer generally. For example, underlying determinants of genetic susceptibility to lung cancer may be more evident in never smokers exposed to second-hand smoke, radon, or other agents than in smokers.

- Research on lung cancer in never smokers has long been hindered by the difficulty in assembling large series, in part because of the need to separate never smokers from the far larger numbers of ever smokers with lung cancer. In most clinical trials, analysis of outcome by smoking status has not been reported.

- Research on lung cancer has been generally underfunded in relation to the burden of morbidity and mortality. Even relative to this baseline, targeted funding to study lung cancer in never smokers has been inadequate.

More Research Is Needed

- Reliable population estimates of incidence and prevalence of lung cancer in never smokers are needed among different ethnic groups, in different countries, and over time.

- Causation in a large fraction of lung cancers in never smokers remains undefined. Research to characterize unidentified and emerging risk factors should continue and should focus on populations likely to be particularly informative, such as cases with early age of onset. . . .

- Studies of genetic determinants of susceptibility in never smokers have been limited and primarily inconclusive. Further research is needed to address candidate genes, including but not limited to those implicated in tobacco carcinogenesis. . . .

- Although exposure questionnaires can be further refined, complementary biomarkers of longer term exposure to lung carcinogens, particularly tobacco smoke, are needed. . . .

- Lung cancers in never smokers with well-characterized exposures should be a focus of future studies of the cancer genome. . . .

- Optimal treatment approaches for never smokers have not been established. . . . Therapeutic trials focused on lung cancer generally should include prospective data collection about never, former, and current smoking status of study participants.

- All studies on lung cancer, regardless of purpose, should include information sufficient to classify study participants by active smoking status (never, current, former) and by exposure to second-hand smoke status.

- To facilitate comparison across studies, a consistent definition of never smoking is needed. On the basis of an emerging consensus of recent and ongoing studies, we support a definition of fewer than 100 lifetime cigarettes smoked. . . .

- An approach to surveillance of lung cancer rates by smoking status (never, current, and former) in the general population in the United States and elsewhere should be established. Coverage should be sufficient to characterize rates by gender and by racial and/or ethnic group. In the United States, this tracking could be accomplished through the National Cancer Institute Surveillance, Epidemiology, and End Results (SEER) program. . . .

- Research on lung cancer in never smokers is hindered by the small numbers of cases available to individual researchers or centers. Mechanisms should be established for facilitating collaborative research on lung cancer in never smokers. . . .

- Recent work has begun to define differences in lung cancer biology associated with smoking status and tobacco exposure. These areas should constitute a continued focus of research, with implications for both lung cancer prevention and lung cancer treatment.

FAST FACT

Utah has the lowest rate of lung cancer among the U.S. states, according to the Centers for Disease Control and Prevention.

Knowledge Will Help Nonsmokers and Smokers, Too

The past decade has been notable for an emerging focus of interest in lung cancer in the never smoker across multiple disciplines including advocacy, epidemiology, clinical medicine, and bench sciences, reflected in increasing numbers of focused research publications addressing this patient population. This trend has been in part driven by a simple clinical observation: never smokers with lung cancer, especially those with EGFR mutations, show preferential benefit from a new class of anti-cancer drugs, the EGFR tyrosine kinase inhibitors. Continued interrogation of the biology of lung cancer in never smokers is likely to reveal additional therapeutic targets of relevance to smokers and never smokers alike.

CHAPTER 2

Controversies Concerning Lung Cancer

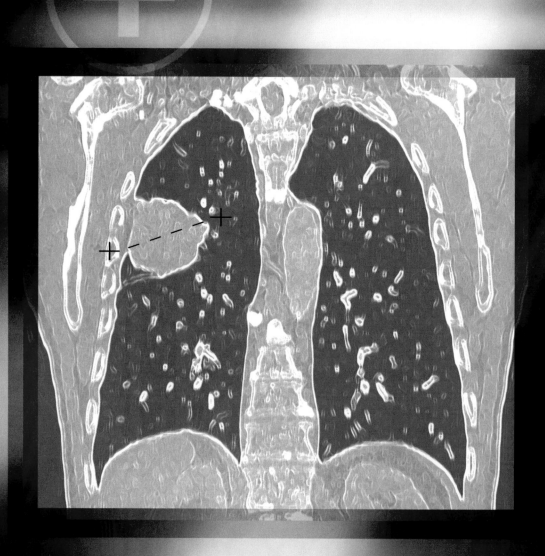

X: 512 Y: 512
W: 2986 L: -167

Marijuana Increases the Risk of Lung Cancer

PR Newswire

The following viewpoint contends that marijuana contains many of the same cancer-causing agents as tobacco. Although the American Lung Association and the American Cancer Society have done well to increase awareness of the health risk posed by tobacco, the former director of National Drug Control Policy, John P. Walters, believes that their success must be built upon in order to educate children on the harms and risks posed by marijuana. Both marijuana and tobacco pose a significant risk for lung cancer. PR Newswire is a leading global vendor in information and news distribution services for professional communicators.

The White House Office of National Drug Control Policy (ONDCP) is adding a new twist to a critical anti-smoking message. Together, with the American Lung Association and the American Cancer

Photo on facing page. This colored computed tomography scan shows a patient with lung cancer. A cancerous tumor (purple) is seen in the right lung. (Miriam Maslo/Photo Researchers, Inc.)

SOURCE: PR Newswire, "American Children in Double Jeopardy: Cigarette and Marijuana Smoke Damaging Young Lungs; Kids Trying Marijuana and Cigarettes in Nearly Equal Proportions; Youth Marijuana Use Exceeds Cigarette Use in Many Major Cities," November 19, 2003. Reproduced by permission.

Society, ONDCP will call attention to the dangers that cigarette and marijuana smoke pose to young lungs. Youth and their parents can access information and resources from ONDCP on preventing youth cigarette and marijuana use.

Smoking remains the nation's leading preventable cause of death and recent surveys indicate that both tobacco and marijuana represent a significant public health threat among youth in particular:

- In 2000, 2.2 million youth under age 18 tried cigarettes for the first time and 2.1 million tried marijuana for the first time.

- In 2002, 17.8 percent of 10th graders reported using marijuana and 17.7 percent of 10th graders reported using cigarettes in the past 30 days.

- More high school students use marijuana than cigarettes in 13 of 14 cities surveyed in the Centers for Disease Control's Youth Risk Behavior Surveillance Survey, including: Boston, Chicago, Dallas, Fort Lauderdale, Los Angeles, Miami, New York, Orlando, Palm Beach, Philadelphia, San Bernardino, San Diego, and San Francisco.

Encourage a Smoke-Free Lifestyle

"Cigarettes and marijuana both put young people in danger," said John P. Walters, [former] Director of National Drug Control Policy. "The American Cancer Society and American Lung Association have made great strides in increasing awareness of the health threat posed by tobacco smoke. We must build upon their success to help inoculate our children against the harms of marijuana."

"The most important message we can send to parents about their kids is that they can and do make a difference," said Dr. John R. Seffrin, CEO of the American Cancer Society. "Parents need to encourage a healthy

Lung Cancer Risk: Marijuana Versus Cigarettes*

One Marijuana Joint = Twenty Cigarettes

*Estimates vary

Taken from: S. Aldington et al. "Cannabis Use and Risk of Lung Cancer: A Case-Controlled Study," *European Respiratory Journal*, February 2008.

and smoke-free lifestyle for their kids. The stakes for our youth are simply too high. There is no such thing as safe inhalation of smoke. Damage is done with the first inhalation and gets worse with each puff taken."

Marijuana smoke contains some of the same cancer-causing compounds as tobacco, sometimes in higher concentrations. In fact, one joint contains as many cancer-causing chemicals as four cigarettes. Research shows that cigarette smoking among youth reduces the rate of lung growth and the level of maximum lung function that can be achieved.

"There are several problems with marijuana use and lung health," said John Kirkwood, President and CEO, American Lung Association. "First are the short term problems—increased cough, mucus production, and high rates of infection. But more seriously, there are long-term consequences of heightened rates for lung cancer. It's a result of 50–70 percent more carcinogenic material in marijuana smoke than in tobacco smoke."

Marijuana smoke contains some of the same cancer-causing compounds as tobacco. (O.DIGIOT/ Alamy)

Parents looking for more information on teen smoking and marijuana use, including warning signs and prevention tools, can visit the National Youth Anti-Drug Media Campaign's Web site at www.TheAntiDrug.com.

The American Lung Association and Eliminating Cancer

The American Cancer Society Great American Smokeout® has been a part of the national effort to reduce and eliminate cigarette smoking. . . . The American Cancer Society is dedicated to eliminating cancer as a major health problem by saving lives, diminishing suffering, and preventing cancer through research, education, advocacy, and service. Founded in 1913, the Society is headquartered in Atlanta and has 15 regional divisions and local offices in 3,400 communities, involving millions of volunteers across the United States. For more information, call 1-800-ACS-2345 or visit www.cancer.org.

Celebrating its 100th anniversary, the American Lung Association works to prevent lung disease and promote lung health. The Lung Association teaches children the dangers of tobacco use and helps teenage and adult smokers overcome addiction. With the generous support of the public, the American Lung Association is "improving life, one breath at a time." For more information about the American Lung Association, call 1-800-LUNG-USA (1-800-586-4872) or log on to www.lung usa.org.

In 1998, with bipartisan support, Congress created the National Youth Anti-Drug Media Campaign with the goal of educating and enabling young people to reject illicit drugs. Unprecedented in size and scope, the Campaign is a strategically integrated communications effort that combines advertising with public communications outreach to deliver anti-drug messages and skills to America's youth, their parents, and other influential adults.

FAST FACT

A study from 2008 found that people who smoke one marijuana joint every day for a year increase their risk of lung cancer by 8 percent.

Marijuana Does Not Increase Lung Cancer Risk

Fred Gardner

In the following viewpoint Fred Gardner maintains that marijuana does not cause lung cancer. According to Gardner, studies by tobacco researcher Donald Tashkin show that marijuana does not lead to an increase in lung cancer. On the contrary, marijuana smoking may even offer protection from lung cancer for those who also smoke tobacco. According to Gardner, the media have largely ignored Tashkin's results, while they have given a great deal of attention to a New Zealand study showing that marijuana increases lung cancer risk. Gardner discusses a talk given by Tashkin in which he criticizes the methodology of the New Zealand study. Gardner is the editor of *O'Shaughnessy's,* the journal of the California Cannabis Research Medical Group.

Smoking Cannabis Does Not Cause Cancer of Lung or Upper Airways, Tashkin Finds; Data Suggest Possible Protective Effect

SOURCE: Fred Gardner, "The Greatest Story Never Told," *Counterpunch,* May 3, 2008. Reproduced by permission.

The story summarized by [the] headline [above] ran in *O'Shaughnessy's* (Autumn 2005), *Counter-Punch*, and the *Anderson Valley Advertiser*. Did we win Pulitzers, dude? No, the story was ignored or buried by the corporate media. It didn't even make the "Project Censored" list of under-reported stories for 2005. "We were even censored by Project Censored," said Tod Mikuriya, who liked his shot of wry.

Researcher Finds No Lung Cancer Risk

It's not that the subject is trivial. One in three Americans will be afflicted with cancer, we are told by the government (as if it's our immutable fate and somehow acceptable). Cancer is the second leading cause of death in the U.S. and lung cancer the leading killer among cancers. You'd think it would have been very big news when UCLA [University of California–Los Angeles] medical school professor Donald Tashkin revealed that components of marijuana smoke— although they damage cells in respiratory tissue—somehow prevent them from becoming malignant. In other words, something in marijuana exerts an anti-cancer effect.

Tashkin has special credibility. He was the lead investigator on studies dating back to the 1970s that identified the components in marijuana smoke that are toxic. It was Tashkin et al who published photomicrographs showing that marijuana smoke damages cells lining the upper airways. It was the Tashkin lab reporting that benzpyrene—a component of tobacco smoke that plays a role in most lung cancers—is especially prevalent in marijuana smoke. It was Tashkin's data documenting that marijuana smokers are more likely than non-smokers to cough, wheeze, and produce sputum.

Tashkin reviewed his findings April 4 [2008] at a conference [at the Asilomar Conference Grounds in Pacific

> **FAST FACT**
>
> According to the University of Michigan, in 2009 about one-third of twelfth graders smoked marijuana.

A study by tobacco researcher Donald Taskin showed that although components of marijuana smoke cause damage in respiratory tissue, marijuana actually exerts an anticancer effect. (© Janine Wiedel Photolibrary/Alamy)

Grove, California] organized by "Patients Out of Time," a reform group devoted to educating doctors and the public (as opposed to lobbying politicians). Some 30 MDs and nurses got continuing medical education credits for attending.

The National Institute on Drug Abuse [NIDA] supported Tashkin's marijuana-related research over the decades and readily gave him a grant to conduct a large, population-based, case-controlled study that would prove definitively that heavy, long-term marijuana use increases the risk of lung and upper-airways cancers. What Tashkin and his colleagues found, however, disproved their hypothesis. . . .

Tashkin's team interviewed 1,212 cancer patients from the Los Angeles County Cancer Surveillance program, matched for age, gender, and neighborhood with 1,040 cancer-free controls. Marijuana use was measured in "joint years" (number of years smoked times number of joints per day). It turned out that increased marijuana use did not result in higher rates of lung and pharyngeal cancer (whereas tobacco smokers were at greater risk the more they smoked). Tobacco smokers who also smoked marijuana were at slightly lower risk of getting lung cancer than tobacco-only smokers.

Findings Were Not Published

These findings were not deemed worthy of publication in *NIDA Notes.* Tashkin reported them at the 2005 meeting of the International Cannabinoid Research Society and they were published in the October 2006 issue of *Cancer Epidemiology Biomarkers & Prevention.* Without a press release from NIDA calling attention to its significance, the assignment editors of America had no idea that "Marijuana Use and the Risk of Lung and Upper Aerodigestive Tract Cancers: Results of a Population-Based Case-Control Study" by Mia Hashibel, Hal Morgenstern, Yan Cui, Donald P. Tashkin, Zuo-Feng Zhang, Wendy Cozen, Thomas M. Mack and Sander Greenland was a blockbuster story.

I suggested to Eric Bailey of the *L.A. Times* that he write up Tashkin's findings—UCLA provided the local angle if the anti-cancer effect wasn't enough. Bailey said his editors wouldn't be interested for some time because he had just filed a marijuana-related piece (about the special rapport Steph Sherer of Americans for Safe Access enjoyed with some old corporado back in Washington, D.C.). The Tashkin scoop is still there for the taking!

Contradictory Study Criticized

Investigators from New Zealand recently got widespread media attention for a study contradicting Tashkin's results. "Heavy cannabis users may be at greater risk of chronic lung disease—including cancer—compared to tobacco smokers," is how BBC News summed up the New Zealanders' findings. The very small size of the study—79 smokers took part, 21 of whom smoked cannabis only—was not held against the authors. As conveyed in the corporate media, the New Zealand study represented the latest word on this important subject (as if science were some kind of tennis match and the truth just gets truthier with every volley).

Tashkin criticized the New Zealanders' methodology in his talk at Asilomar: "There's some cognitive dissonance associated with the interpretation of their findings. I think this has to do with the belief model among the investigators and—I wish they were here to defend themselves—the integrity of the investigators. . . . They actually published another paper in which they mimicked the design that we used for looking at lung function."

Tashkin spoke from the stage of an airy redwood chapel designed by Julia Morgan [an American architect]. He is pink-cheeked, 70ish, wears wire-rimmed spectacles. "For tobacco they found what you'd expect: a higher risk for lung cancer and a clear dose-response relationship. A 24-fold increase in the people who smoked the most. . . . What about marijuana? If they smoked a small or moderate amount there was no increased risk, in fact slightly less than one. But if they were in the upper third of the group, then their risk was six-fold. . . . A rather surprising finding, and one has to be cautious about interpreting the results because of the very small number of cases (14) and controls (4)."

Tashkin said the New Zealanders employed "statistical sleight of hand." He deemed it "completely implausible that smokers of only 365 joints of marijuana have a risk for developing lung cancer similar to that of smokers of 7,000 tobacco cigarettes. . . . Their small sample size led to vastly inflated estimates. . . . They had said 'it's ideal to do the study in New Zealand because we have a much higher prevalence of marijuana smoking.' But 88 percent of their controls had never smoked marijuana, whereas 36% of our controls (in Los Angeles) had never smoked marijuana. Why did so few of the controls smoke marijuana? Something fishy about that!"

Strong words for a UCLA School of Medicine professor!

Marijuana May Even Help Prevent Lung Cancer

As to the highly promising implication of his own study—that something in marijuana stops damaged cells from becoming malignant—Tashkin noted that an anti-proliferative effect of THC [tetrahydrocannabinol

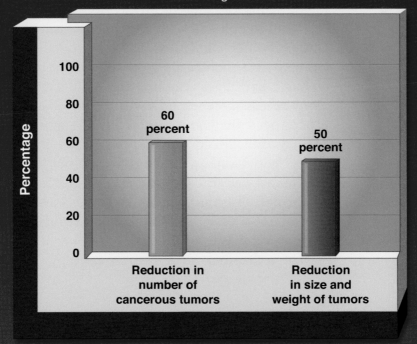

THC* and Tumors

A study with mice shows that THC, the active ingredient in marijuana, reduces the number and size of lung cancer tumors.

*Tetrahydrocannabinol, or THC, is a chemical compound that is the primary intoxicant in marijuana.

Taken from: American Association for Cancer Research, "Marijuana Cuts Lung Cancer Tumor Growth in Half, Study Shows," April 17, 2007. Retrieved from Science Daily, March 5, 2010.

(THC) is the psycho-active ingredient in marijuana] has been observed in cell-culture systems and animal models of brain, breast, prostate, and lung cancer. THC has been shown to promote known apoptosis (damaged cells die instead of reproducing) and to counter angiogenesis (the process by which blood vessels are formed—a requirement of tumor growth). Other antioxidants in cannabis may also be involved in countering malignancy, said Tashkin.

Much of Tashkin's talk was devoted to Chronic Obstructive Pulmonary Disease [COPD], another condition prevalent among tobacco smokers. Chronic bronchitis and emphysema are two forms of COPD, which is the fourth leading cause of death in the United States. Air pollution and tobacco smoke are known culprits. Inhaled pathogens cause an inflammatory response, resulting in diminished lung function. COPD patients have increasing difficulty clearing the airways as they get older.

Tashkin and colleagues at UCLA conducted a major study in which they measured lung function of various cohorts over eight years and found that tobacco-only smokers had an accelerated rate of decline, but marijuana smokers—even if they smoked tobacco as well—experienced the same rate of decline as non-smokers. "The more tobacco smoked, the greater the rate of decline," said Tashkin. "In contrast, no matter how much marijuana was smoked, the rate of decline was similar to normal." Tashkin concluded that his and other studies "do not support the concept that regular smoking of marijuana leads to COPD."

Hope that makes you breathe easier.

CT Screening Can Prevent Lung Cancer Deaths

International Early Lung Cancer Action Project

In the following viewpoint researchers from the International Early Lung Cancer Action Project contend that computerized tomography (CT) screening for lung cancer can dramatically save lives. The researchers undertook a study to determine if routine screening of current and former smokers could detect lung cancer at an early enough stage that it could be successfully treated. Typically, lung cancer survival rates are very low because symptoms do not occur until cancerous tumors are well established and thus difficult to treat. According to the researchers, the lives of hundreds of people were saved because CT screening caught their lung cancer at an early enough stage for a successful outcome. The International Early Lung Cancer Action Project is an international group of lung cancer experts based at Weill Medical College of Cornell University.

SOURCE: International Early Lung Cancer Action Project, "Landmark Study Reveals That Lung Cancer 10-Year Survival Dramatically Improves with Annual CT Screening and Prompt Treatment," October 26, 2006. Reproduced by permission.

Lung cancer can be detected at its very earliest stage in 85 percent of patients using annual low-dose CT [computerized tomography] screening, and when followed by prompt surgical removal the 10-year survival rate is 92 percent. These results, . . . reported in the October 26 [2006] *New England Journal of Medicine*, would dramatically decrease the number of deaths from lung cancer—the number one cause of cancer deaths among both men and women in the U.S.

The study was launched by a team of researchers at New York–Presbyterian Hospital/Weill Cornell Medical Center in 1993 and has expanded into an international collaboration of 38 institutions in 7 countries, the International Early Lung Cancer Action Project (I-ELCAP). The I-ELCAP study is the largest, long-term study to determine the usefulness of annual screening by CT.

FAST FACT

About two out of three people diagnosed with lung cancer are older than sixty-five; fewer than 3 percent of all cases are found in people younger than forty-five, according to the American Cancer Society.

Early Detection Crucial for Saving Lives

Stage I lung cancer is the only stage at which cure by surgery is highly likely. While survival rates have been climbing for other forms of cancer, the survival rates for lung cancer have remained dismal. Approximately 95 percent of the 173,000 people diagnosed each year die from the disease—more than breast, prostate and colon cancer combined. The high death rates are a consequence of lung cancer not being detected early enough for treatment to be curative.

Among the 31,567 people in the study, CT screening detected 484 people who were diagnosed with lung cancer, 412 of these were Stage I. Of the Stage I patients who chose not to be treated, all died within five years. Overall, the estimated 10-year survival rate for the 484 participants with lung cancer was 80 percent. The participants were 40 years of age and

American Cancer Society Recommendations for the Early Detection of Cancer in Average Risk, Asymptomatic Individuals

Type of Cancer	Test	Who Should Be Screened and How Often?
Breast	Mammography	Women 40 and over, annually
Colorectal	Fecal occult blood test	Men and women 50 and over, annually
	Sigmoidoscopy	Men and women 50 and over, every 5 years
Prostate	Rectal exam and prostate-specific antigen (PSA) test	Offer to men 50 and over
Cervix	Pap test	Women 18 and over, annually

Taken from: American Cancer Society, "Cancer Prevention & Early Detection Facts & Figures," 2009. www.cancer.org.

older and at risk for lung cancer because of a history of cigarette smoking, occupational exposure (to asbestos, beryllium, uranium or radon), or exposure to second-hand smoke.

"We believe this study provides compelling evidence that CT screening for lung cancer offers new hope for millions of people at risk for this disease and could dramatically reverse lung cancer death rates," said Dr. Claudia Henschke, the study's lead author and principal investigator who is chief of the chest imaging division at New York–Presbyterian/Weill Cornell and professor of radiology and cardiothoracic surgery at Weill Cornell Medical College.

Technological Advances

Since the early 1990s, there have been remarkable advances in CT scanners. Sub-millimeter "slicing" can now be applied to the entire chest in a single breath-hold. As a result, lung cancer may be detected when it is smaller than it was possible to diagnose previously. Although CT scans once yielded only 30 images, current technology

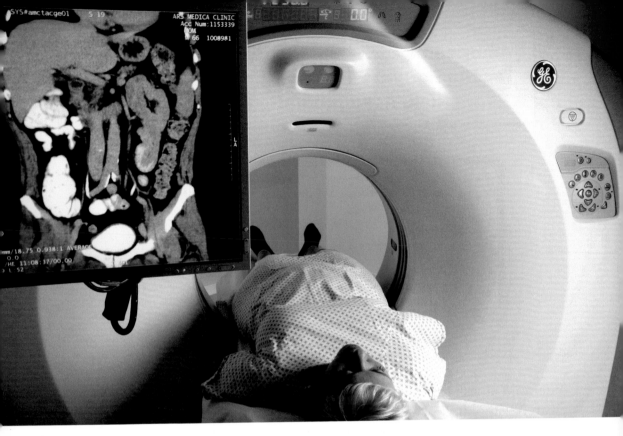

The authors contend that the use of computerized tomography screening can dramatically increase the likelihood of detecting lung cancer early. (Mauro Fermariello/Photo Researchers, Inc.)

yields over 600 images. As the technology advanced, the approaches for studying the usefulness of this technology have also advanced.

The charge for a low-dose CT screening varies, but ranges from $200 to $300. Treatment for Stage I lung cancer is less than half the cost of late-stage treatment. Estimates of the cost-effectiveness of CT screening for lung cancer are similar or better than those for mammography screening for breast cancer.

CT Screening for Lung Cancer May Not Be Effective

Matthew B. Stanbrook and Ken Flegel

In the following viewpoint Matthew B. Stanbrook and Ken Flegel provide several reasons why computed tomography (CT) screening may not be effective at preventing lung cancer. Stanbrook and Flegel assert that the dramatic results of the International Early Lung Cancer Action Project study—where lung cancer was detected at its earliest stages in 85 percent of patients—may be exaggerated. They also question the effectiveness of other kinds of cancer screening, including tests for prostate and breast cancer. Stanbrook and Flegel believe there are better, more cost-effective ways to prevent lung cancer than CT screening. Stanbrook is a professor in the Health Policy, Management, and Evaluation Department at the University of Toronto. Flegel is a professor of medicine at McGill University and a senior editor for the *Canadian Medical Association Journal*.

More effective clinical strategies are badly needed to combat lung cancer, the leading cause of both cancer incidence and cancer death. A novel screening strategy based on low-dose computed tomography (CT) scanning is being studied in large randomized trials and may hold promise. However, the wide availability of CT threatens to undermine evidence-based practice if clinicians are inappropriately hasty in adopting CT screening. In our practices, we regularly encounter patients who inquire about or have already undergone CT-based screening. Some patient advocacy groups, such as the US Lung Cancer Alliance, have promoted this type of screening.

Advances in CT technology now permit imaging at sufficient resolution to identify lung nodules as small as a few millimetres in diameter while exposing patients to lower doses of radiation than would be required for a conventional thoracic CT scan. The largest and most prominent study to date of CT-based screening for lung cancer, the International Early Lung Cancer Action Project (I-ELCAP), has reported that screening with low-dose CT can successfully identify curable lung cancer at an early stage. The I-ELCAP protocol involved screening at baseline and annually thereafter. New nodules identified were investigated within a defined algorithm [process] incorporating frequent CT scans, positron emission tomography [PET] scans, antibiotics or lung biopsy. Patients found to have cancer underwent surgical resection; the 10-year survival rate for these patients was 88%–92%.

Reasons Not to Rush into Screening

Given such favourable results, why shouldn't we rush to embrace CT-based screening for lung cancer? First, screening brings with it important unintended consequences. In the I-ELCAP study, screening was inefficient, identifying cancers in only 1.3% of participants. Other abnormalities, which were ultimately found to be benign but that required further workup, were 10-fold more common. Although the I-ELCAP protocol prevented unnecessary biopsies, patients were subjected to unnecessary anxiety while awaiting further testing.

However, an even more important consideration is that the apparent success demonstrated in CT screening studies for lung cancer may be an illusion. Screening for cancer is prone to several well-described types of bias, each of which could account for the study findings. The need to find cancers when they are small, although seemingly important, does not match the biology of all

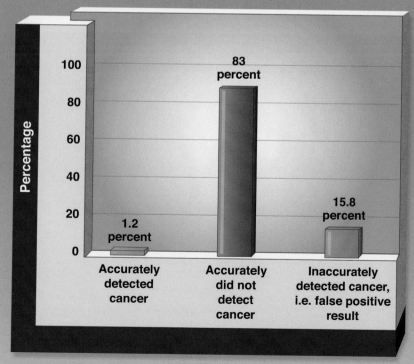

Detecting Lung Cancer

CT and chest X-Ray lung cancer screens of current and former smokers often produce a high rate of false positives.

Taken from: Roxanne Nelson, "ASCO 2009: Low-Dose CT Screening for Lung Cancer Produces High Rate of False Positives," *Medscape Today*, June 4, 2009.

tumours. Rather than identifying cancers for which the potential for cure would otherwise have been missed, screening may merely provide earlier identification of cancers that remain curable after becoming clinically apparent (lead-time bias). Although screening increases the number of cancers diagnosed, many are slow-growing, indolent tumours (length-time bias). For some patients, screening may lead to overdiagnosis and overtreatment of cancers that would never become clinically evident because death from another cause is far more likely.

Clinicians ought to know better than to leap too early on the cancer screening bandwagon. We have been here before. Chest radiographs and sputum cytology [looking at phlegm under a microscope to search for cancer cells] were found to be ineffective screening tools for lung cancer after many years of research. Prostate-specific antigen testing is widespread in clinical practice, yet it has never been proven to reduce mortality from prostate cancer. Although a beneficial effect of mammography has been

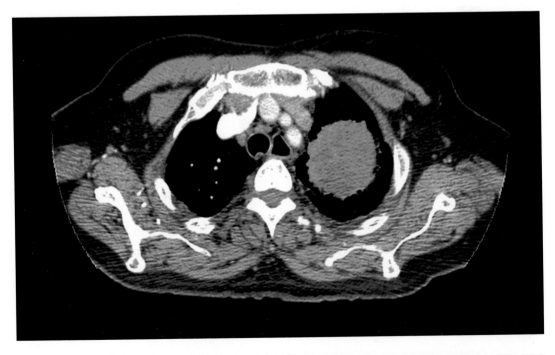

A large cancerous mass (green) is shown in this computed tomography (CT) scan of a chest. Some experts have questioned the validity of CT scans, arguing that they can sometimes lead to overdiagnosis and overtreatment of cancers. (**Medical Body Scans/Photo Researchers, Inc.**)

proven in older women, whether it reduces mortality from breast cancer in women aged 40–49 years is unknown. This highlights the consequences of failure to define optimal population subgroups for screening.

We acknowledge that proponents of CT screening may be right about its benefits. However, benefits need to be proven rather than assumed. The opportunity for proof will be lost if we allow premature enthusiasm to disseminate into widespread practice.

Better Ways to Prevent Lung Cancer

National and international professional organizations representing cancer, lung disease and medical imaging specialists could help by collaborating on joint policy statements to guide practice in the interim. Until then, if clinicians choose to offer CT screening for lung cancer, such decisions should be based on their best judgment of the incomplete evidence available and on the values and preferences of their patients, with forthright acknowledgement of the present uncertainty. Ideally, such patients should be enrolled in clinical trials of CT screening. Similarly, policy-makers should wait for better evidence of efficacy and cost-effectiveness before investing in more capacity for CT screening programs. In the meantime, given how much we know about the prevention of lung cancer, targeting smoking avoidance and cessation, rather than detection and management of lung cancer, would seem a better investment.

> **FAST FACT**
>
> According to the National Cancer Institute, about 25 to 60 percent of CT scans of smokers and former smokers will show abnormalities that are not cancer.

Secondhand Smoke Causes Lung Cancer and Other Adverse Health Effects

National Cancer Institute

In the following viewpoint the National Cancer Institute (NCI) asserts that secondhand smoke is dangerous. According to the institute, secondhand smoke contains a multitude of harmful chemicals that cause lung cancer and heart disease and that may cause strokes and many other cancers. The NCI says that there is no safe level of secondhand smoke exposure, and the only way to protect non-smokers from the dangers of secondhand smoke is to eliminate smoking in all indoor spaces. The National Cancer Institute is the U.S. government's principal agency for cancer research and one of the twenty-seven institutes and centers that compose the National Institutes of Health.

Q: *What is secondhand smoke?*

A: Secondhand smoke (also called environmental tobacco smoke) is the combination of sidestream smoke (the smoke given off by the burning end of a tobacco product) and mainstream smoke (the

SOURCE: National Cancer Institute Factsheet, "Secondsmoke: Questions and Answers," August 1, 2007.

smoke exhaled by the smoker). Exposure to secondhand smoke is also called involuntary smoking or passive smoking. People are exposed to secondhand smoke in homes, cars, the workplace, and public places such as bars, restaurants, and other recreation settings. In the United States, the source of most secondhand smoke is from cigarettes, followed by pipes, cigars, and other tobacco products.

Q: How is secondhand smoke exposure measured?

A: Secondhand smoke is measured by testing indoor air for nicotine or other smoke constituents. Exposure to secondhand smoke can be tested by measuring the levels of cotinine (a nicotine by-product in the body) in the nonsmoker's blood, saliva, or urine. Nicotine, cotinine, carbon monoxide, and other evidence of secondhand smoke exposure have been found in the body fluids of nonsmokers exposed to secondhand smoke.

Q: Does secondhand smoke contain harmful chemicals?

A: Yes. Of the more than 4,000 chemicals that have been identified in secondhand tobacco smoke, at least 250 are known to be harmful, and 50 of these are known to cause cancer. These chemicals include:

- arsenic (a heavy metal toxin)
- benzene (a chemical found in gasoline)
- beryllium (a toxic metal)
- cadmium (a metal used in batteries)
- chromium (a metallic element)
- ethylene oxide (a chemical used to sterilize medical devices)
- nickel (a metallic element)
- polonium-210 (a chemical element that gives off radiation)
- vinyl chloride (a toxic substance used in plastics manufacture)

Secondhand Smoke Is Toxic

Secondhand smoke has more than 4,000 chemicals. Many of these chemicals are toxic and cause cancer. You breathe in these chemicals when you are around someone who is smoking.

A sampling of chemicals in cigarette smoke:		
Ammonia	Cadmium	Hydrogen cyanide
Arsenic	Carbon monoxide	Lead
Benzene	Chromium	Polonium-210
Butane	Formaldehyde	Vinyl chloride

Taken from: Office on Smoking and Health, National Center for Chronic Disease Prevention and Health Promotion, Centers for Disease Control and Prevention.

Many factors affect which chemicals are found in secondhand smoke, including the type of tobacco, the chemicals added to the tobacco, the way the product is smoked, and the paper in which the tobacco is wrapped.

Harmful Effects of Secondhand Smoke Exposure

Q: Does exposure to secondhand smoke cause cancer?

A: Yes. The U.S. Environmental Protection Agency (EPA), the U.S. National Toxicology Program (NTP), the U.S. surgeon general, and the International Agency for Research on Cancer (IARC) have classified secondhand smoke as a known human carcinogen (cancer-causing agent).

Inhaling secondhand smoke causes lung cancer in nonsmoking adults. Approximately 3,000 lung cancer deaths occur each year among adult nonsmokers in the United States as a result of exposure to secondhand smoke. The surgeon general estimates that living with a

PERSPECTIVES ON DISEASES AND DISORDERS

smoker increases a nonsmoker's chances of developing lung cancer by 20 to 30 percent.

Some research suggests that secondhand smoke may increase the risk of breast cancer, nasal sinus cavity cancer, and nasopharyngeal [the upper part of the throat]

Children exposed to secondhand smoke are at increased risk of sudden infant death syndrome, ear infections, colds, pneumonia, bronchitis, and asthma. (**Olivier Voisin/ Photo Researchers, Inc.**)

cancer in adults, and leukemia [cancer of the blood or bone marrow], lymphoma [cancer affecting the immune system], and brain tumors in children. Additional research is needed to learn whether a link exists between secondhand smoke exposure and these cancers.

Q: What are the other health effects of exposure to secondhand smoke?

A: Secondhand smoke causes disease and premature death in nonsmoking adults and children. Exposure to secondhand smoke irritates the airways and has immediate harmful effects on a person's heart and blood vessels. It may increase the risk of heart disease by an estimated 25 to 30 percent. In the United States, secondhand smoke is thought to cause about 46,000 heart disease deaths each year. There may also be a link between exposure to secondhand smoke and the risk of stroke and hardening of the arteries; however, additional research is needed to confirm this link.

Children exposed to secondhand smoke are at an increased risk of sudden infant death syndrome (SIDS), ear infections, colds, pneumonia, bronchitis, and more severe asthma. Being exposed to secondhand smoke slows the growth of children's lungs and can cause them to cough, wheeze, and feel breathless.

Q: What is a safe level of secondhand smoke?

A: There is no safe level of exposure to secondhand smoke. Studies have shown that even low levels of secondhand smoke exposure can be harmful. The only way to fully protect nonsmokers from secondhand smoke exposure is to completely eliminate smoking in indoor spaces. Separating smokers from nonsmokers, cleaning the air, and ventilating buildings cannot completely eliminate secondhand smoke exposure.

Q: What is being done to reduce nonsmokers' exposure to secondhand smoke?

FAST FACT

Each year in the United States, more never smokers die of lung cancer than do patients with leukemia, ovarian cancer, or AIDS, according to a review published in the journal *Nature* in 2006.

A: Many state and local governments have passed laws prohibiting smoking in public facilities such as schools, hospitals, airports, and bus terminals. Increasingly, state and local governments are also requiring private workplaces, including restaurants and bars, to be smoke free. To highlight the significant risk from secondhand smoke exposure, the National Cancer Institute, a component of the National Institutes of Health, holds meetings and conferences in states, counties, cities, or towns that are smoke free, unless certain circumstances justify an exception to this policy.

The Dangers of Secondhand Smoke Are Overstated

John Stossel

In the following viewpoint John Stossel argues that the dangers of secondhand smoke are exaggerated. According to Stossel, studies on the dangers of secondhand smoke were carried out by following nonsmokers who were constantly exposed to heavy smokers in cramped quarters. Stossel says this is not the kind of secondhand smoke exposure most people experience. Stossel thinks that antismoking groups are distorting the real risks of secondhand smoke exposure to support their crusade to ban smoking everywhere, even outside and in people's own apartments. Stossel is an investigative reporter. He has worked for ABC News and Fox News.

S econdhand smoke—even a little is a killer. It's why more of you smokers are banned from bars, restaurants, now even building entrances.

One public service announcement proclaims, "When you smoke, you're not the only one being harmed."

SOURCE: John Stossel, "Myth: Secondhand Smoke Is a Killer," ABC News: *20/20*, May 3, 2007. Reproduced by permission.

That's not a myth. Studies that followed nonsmokers who lived with smokers found some increase in lung cancer and heart disease. But they studied people who were exposed to lots of smoke, often shut in with chain smokers for years in claustrophobic situations like homes and cars. Even then, some of the studies found no effect. Nevertheless it's been enough to launch a movement to ban smoking most everywhere.

And now Calabasas, Calif., has banned smoking everywhere outdoors where a nonsmoker could get within 20 feet of a smoker. The former mayor, Barry Groveman, said, "It's about public safety."

"This is by every standard a public health law," Groveman said.

How Big Is the Risk?

But if they limit people's choices in the name of public health, we should know if walking past a smoker can really hurt you. I fell for the alarmists' claims years ago when I interviewed activist Stanton Glantz about secondhand smoke.

"And if I were to walk up to you and have an aerosol can filled with 4,000 chemicals and say, 'Excuse me, do you mind if I spray this in your face,' you'd think I was out of my mind, but when somebody smokes a cigarette, that's what they're doing," Glantz said.

Glantz and other activists now say just 20 or 30 minutes of smoke puts you on the road to a deadly heart attack.

> **FAST FACT**
>
> According to the World Health Organization, almost 1 billion men in the world smoke—about 35 percent of men in developed countries and 50 percent of men in developing countries.

Dr. Michael Siegel, a leading advocate of bans on smoking in the workplace because of the harm from daily exposure to secondhand smoke, says the 20 or 30 minute claims are ridiculous.

"If someone is just exposed for 30 minutes, it's completely reversible, and it's not gonna cause hardening of the arteries," Siegel said.

Siegel, who helped ban smoking in restaurants and bars, now says his movement is distorting science.

The Crusade

"It has turned into more of a crusade," Siegel said. "The cause has kind of taken over."

Some anti-smoking advocates want it banned even inside apartments.

"Now people are complaining about smoke going from one apartment to another apartment," Glantz said.

States That Have and Have Not Established Smoking Bans

All but eleven states have instituted full or partial smoking bans in public places.

States that ban smoking in some or all public places

States that have enacted no smoking ban of any kind

[Compiled by the editor.]

Unlike these antismoking demonstrators, critics of smoking bans argue that the effects of secondhand smoke are exaggerated. (AP Images)

Glantz said the people in other apartments could be harmed since the "level of toxicity in the smoke is very very high."

Frankly, I like the smoke-free zones, but the science behind them may be a myth.

"I think the documented health effects of secondhand smoke are enough. I don't think we need to be stretching the truth," Siegel said.

CHAPTER 3

Personal Experiences with Lung Cancer

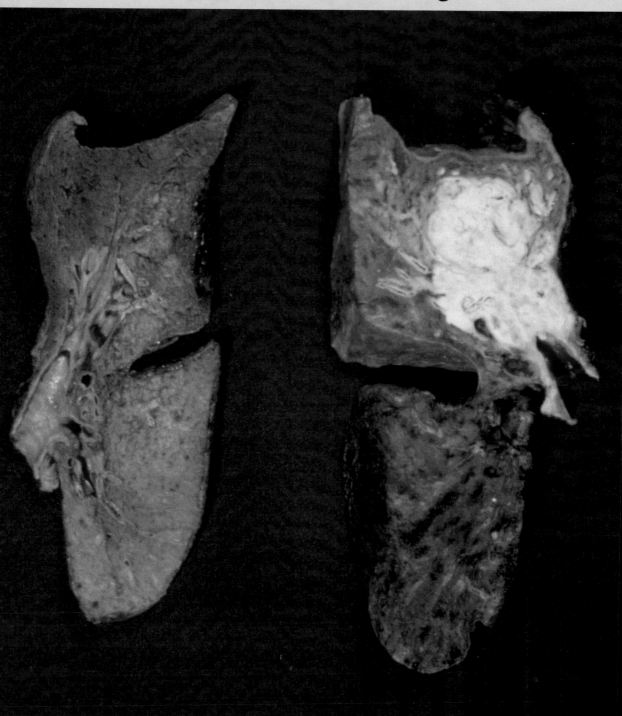

Living with Cancer and Facing Death

Michael Kirwan

In the following viewpoint Michael Kirwan relays his grim prognosis in a letter to friends and supporters. Kirwan documents his undying faith in his letter and expresses gratitude. Although his lung cancer spread throughout his body, Kirwan did not fear death and was willing to do whatever God had in store for him.

Michael Kirwan died of cancer on November 12, 1999. He was fifty-four. For over twenty years, he lived with the poor in Washington, D.C., founding two Catholic Worker houses in the inner city and a farm in West Virginia. A life-long reader of *Commonweal,* a Catholic periodical, Kirwan sent the following letter on September 8—here abridged—to friends and benefactors.

L ast Tuesday, my doctor at Providence Hospital told me the cancer within my lung had spread. It is now in my brain, colon, liver, elbow, foot, hip, and leg. There is not much to be done except to pray. The doctor said it would take a miracle to put me well again.

SOURCE: Michael Kirwan, "Going Forth (Michael Kirwan Leaves Letter After Dying from Cancer)," *Commonweal,* December 3, 1999. Reproduced by permission of Commonweal Foundation.

Photo on facing page. Post-mortem specimens show a normal lung, left, and one destroyed by lung cancer. In the latter, the white area is a cancerous tumor; the blackened area is the result of cigarette smoking. (St Bartholomew's Hospital/Photo Researchers, Inc.)

Otherwise, I can expect to live from one to six months—shorter rather than longer—since the cancer has become very aggressive.

I don't pray for a miracle. Rather, I pray that I will do whatever God has in store for me. I pray for the women and men of my family who are deeply grieved, and I am especially praying for the people of our farm and houses on the streets, where there is much fear and anxiety over the ceasing of a long and caring association. I know that it will not cease but rather be changed. As my work ebbs, other work commences.

We cannot by ourselves lift the burden of racism, economic and social disparity, suspicion and mistrust; but we can begin to lighten it. Our responses are always an attempt: a small mustard seed of faith to grow, to nurture, to plant again that others might sow and reap. Our response to the gospel is different in all of our lives. Whatever leads to God must be counted as valid.

Faith Continues

My own journey began with my parents and their attraction to a gospel that called for personalism, the intimacy of faith in action that was exemplified in the lives of Dorothy Day and Peter Maurin. That continues. Again and again, over these years, men and women who came into my life seeking hospitality stayed on to provide it. Groups of young people who were briefly touched by the experience of living among the poor came back again. So the work moves from one generation to another. We will never know completely where our influence has touched, but God has worked with the few loaves and a couple of fish and done the rest.

I do not fear death. I fear not being a good and faithful friend and of not being filled with gratitude and joy to a good and gracious God who has so favored me with grace in my unworthiness. God has chosen someone weak and strengthened him. I have seen it in my own life countless times, and in the lives of so many who came across my path.

I think and pray now with all of you and ask that you always remember me as someone who tried to do the best he could and, on not-so-good days, tried to do better. I always tried to break down barriers and build friendships and peace; I trusted that God would see things to completion in good time. I still believe that with all my heart and soul. God will provide, especially now.

> **FAST FACT**
>
> More than 400,000 people alive today have been diagnosed with lung cancer at some point, according to the American Cancer Society.

I might add that I have not thrown in the towel. For the moment, I am able to manage fairly well and rejoice in the normal operation of the houses. Our work goes on as always. One of the men in our house on T Street went out last night to the parks instead of me, with water, clothes, blankets, toilet articles, and meal tickets. Today our soup line opened and people came in to take showers and use the phone. Hospitality continues. Love goes on. I may not be able to write you again, but my family will be ever vigilant and let all of you know what is happening.

To you, our friends and generous benefactors, I want to especially express my heartfelt gratitude for your faithful trust and prayers. Some have told me that I am the "glue" that holds these houses and this work together. But God is the real unifying force and God will see to it that these places and this work continue, perhaps in a somewhat changed form. For now, let us rejoice and be glad. Emmanuel, the Lord is with us! Love, prayers, and gratitude.

The Price of Smoking for Fifty Years

David W. Cowles

In the following viewpoint inventor and businessman David W. Cowles tells of his experience with smoking and subsequently developing lung cancer. Cowles tried his first cigarette at the age of fifteen and continued to smoke for fifty years. After a routine medical exam, Cowles's doctor determined that he had emphysema and lung cancer. Cowles was lucky to discover his cancer when he did. If he had gone to the doctor a few months later, the cancer might have already spread to the lymph nodes. Although Cowles admits he truly enjoyed smoking, he wishes he had found his pleasure elsewhere.

I finally kicked the habit after 50 years, but I couldn't escape lung cancer and emphysema.

I'm not going to waste your time trying to persuade you to quit smoking. You've already heard or read all of the reasons that you shouldn't light up. You're seen the surgeon general's warnings on every pack of cigarettes and in every tobacco ad. You've been lectured by

SOURCE: David W. Cowles, "The Price of Smoking," *Newsweek,* February 1, 1999. Reproduced by permission.

friends and family. You're aware that more people die from lung cancer than from breast cancer, prostate cancer and colorectal cancer combined—and that almost all lung cancer is caused by smoking.

The fact is, until you're ready to break the habit, none of the arguments proffered by antismoking advocates will have even the slightest impact. But, since you've read this far, I'll give you the benefit of my experiences.

Getting Hooked on Cigarettes

I tried my first cigarette when I was 15. Always a scrawny kid, I thought that smoking made me look more adult and sophisticated and therefore more attractive to the opposite sex. Plus, I liked the slightly intoxicated buzz that inhaling provided. Before long, I was hooked and smoking a pack a day.

Fifty years later, I still enjoyed cigarettes. With my morning coffee. After a good meal. Relaxing in front of a video-poker machine at my favorite Las Vegas casino. I'd even joke about nonsmokers, asking what they did after having sex.

My cardiologist tried his best to persuade me to stop. He said I'd reduce the risk of having a heart attack or stroke, lower my blood pressure and improve my circulation. I felt that he was probably right—for other people. After all, my father had smoked all of his life and lived to his 90s. I would listen politely, eager for the good doctor to finish so that I could get out to my car and light up.

On numerous occasions I halfheartedly tried to quit. Not because I really wanted to, but because it seemed to be the right thing to do. Sometimes my determination lasted less than an hour before I absolutely had to have a cigarette.

Smoking Affects Health

Much as I didn't want to admit it, for the last couple of years I knew that smoking was affecting my health. I'd be out of breath after climbing a short flight of stairs and had great difficulty keeping pace with my companions in the mile-high air of the Utah mountains where we went trout fishing every Father's Day.

Things got particularly acute this past summer. I'd installed a small fish pond in my backyard, and every week I had to clean out the water filter. Just bending over to open the filter unit wore me out. I'd come back into the house gasping for breath, sit down and smoke several cigarettes until I mustered up the energy to finish the chore.

One night I was on my way home from work when I realized that I was down to three cigarettes. I could stop at a store and buy a carton, or . . . pick up a box of nicotine patches. While I read the instructions, I smoked my last cigarette.

I quickly discovered the two distinct components of the smoking habit: the nicotine addiction and the situational desires. I'll give the patches full credit for alleviating the nervousness and irritability that cold-turkey nicotine withdrawal causes.

The situational aspects of smoking were far more difficult to overcome. When I climbed out of bed, drove off in my car or waited to be served in a restaurant, I automatically reached to my shirt pocket. The smoking habit was deeply entrenched and died very hard indeed.

The results? Within 24 hours, I was not nearly as short of breath. Within days, the morning hacking and spitting up was greatly reduced. At six weeks, I climbed all 91 steps to the top of Kukulkan Pyramid in Chichén Itzá, Mexico.

The Results of Fifty Years of Smoking

But 50 years of smoking took their toll. During a routine medical exam last November [1998], my internist determined that I had emphysema. And that wasn't all. An

> **FAST FACT**
>
> According to the National Cancer Institute, there were an estimated 219,440 new cases of lung cancer diagnosed in 2009.

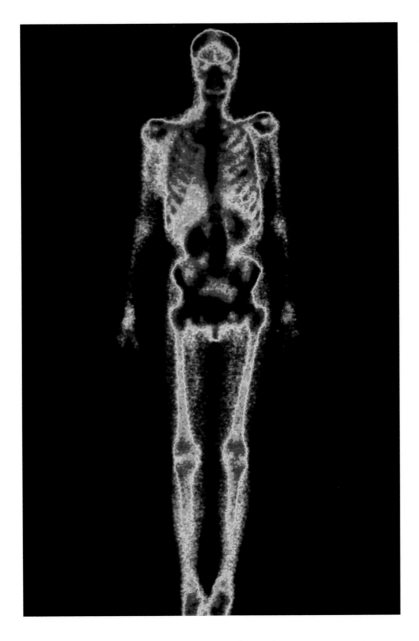

A positron emission tomography scan shows that cancer has spread to a patient's ribs and vertebra. **(Scott Carmazine/Photo Researchers, Inc.)**

X-ray revealed a spot on one of my lungs. A CAT scan showed it to be a marble-size tumor.

The cardiovascular surgeon postulated that there was a 65 percent chance the tumor was malignant and only 35 percent that it was benign. He recommended an immediate biopsy, with more radical surgery should the tumor prove to be malignant.

I was admitted to the hospital exactly four months from the day I quit smoking. The tumor turned out to be a stage-one squamous cell carcinoma—a type of lung cancer strongly related to smoking. The surgeon removed the tumor and a lobe of one lung.

He told me afterward that I was fortunate. If I had had my physical exam a few months earlier, the tumor might not have been discovered. A few months later, and the cancer might have already spread to the lymph nodes or metastasized elsewhere. The surgeon was confident that all of the cancer had been excised and that there would be no recurrence.

But I felt anything but lucky. For days after the operation I was in such horrendous pain I believed I'd never leave the hospital alive. For more than a month the excruciating pain continued. Even now, I am still very short of breath.

Yes, I genuinely enjoyed smoking. But I certainly wish that I had found my pleasure elsewhere.

The Injustice
of Lung Cancer

Lisa Bowen

In the following excerpts from her diary, Lisa Bowen, a thirty-eight-year-old Australian mother of three, shares her inner thoughts as she battles with an incurable form of lung cancer. Bowen, like most of us, thought that nothing bad in the world could happen to her. But her world changed when she—a nonsmoker—found a lump on her neck and weeks later received a diagnosis of stage IV lung cancer. The doctors told her that her cancer was incurable and any treatment she received would be only to prolong her life. Bowen shares her sadness and anger at not being able to see her children grow up and for having her life taken from her. Bowen died in the arms of her husband on July 4, 2007, three weeks after her last journal entry.

I had a thought one day. What if the world really did revolve around me? What if everything that happens around me happens because I dream it into existence? Every event and every person I know. That would be why nothing bad ever happens to me. I can get into

SOURCE: Lisa Bowen, "I Had a Thought One Day," Kylie Johnston Lung Cancer Network, 2007, pp. 3–5, 15–16, 28, 30–31. Reproduced by permission.

bad scrapes and have lots of close calls, but I always manage to come out on top. It was just a thought.

Bad things always happen to other people. I have never lost anyone close to me. No one I know has ever been tragically ill. My children are well. Of course I take all this for granted. I can't help it. It's just the way it is. You take things for granted that are always there. There's no reason not to.

My World Turned Upside Down

And then my world turned upside down. Christmas 2005, I was 36 years old. A few days before Christmas I was sitting in my comfy chair watching TV. Relaxed. Kids in bed. I rubbed my neck and noticed a large lump under my skin. I didn't think much of it, but got my husband to feel it who just shrugged it off. I decided to go to the doctor to check it out but it was Christmas so it could wait. It was a great Christmas, and it wasn't till a few days after Christmas I managed to find some time to go to the doctor who suggested an ultrasound. Probably a cyst or something like that. Don't worry. I didn't. Booking in for an ultrasound over the Christmas/New Year break proved impossible so it was over a week before I actually got it done. I took three kids with me that day as Andrew my husband was at the cricket match [a ball game]. I lined the three of them up with their Nintendo DS's in the waiting room and in I went.

I was told to go to my GP [general practitioner] straight away and not to wait till tomorrow. I guess the first stages of panic started then. Also the kids had completely had enough by now, so I wasn't getting much sympathy from the gallery. After an hour waiting for the doctor I finally found out I had at least 6 enlarged lymph glands and that I possibly had something called "Lymphoma." Not to worry. Some chemo and maybe all will be well. I didn't really get too many details as my three kids sounded like they were trying to kill each other waiting [outside] the door and I couldn't concentrate at all on what was being said. However we did manage to plan a biopsy and some blood tests.

At least after that point I managed to have some help with the kids, but that day was certainly a long one. Yet you think things couldn't possibly ever get any worse, and then as you go they do. I started having problems breathing as the lymph nodes were putting pressure on my airways. After the biopsy things seemed to start growing even faster.

Next thing I know I am in the hospital, can't breathe, and know after a CT [computed tomography] scan that I seem to have a barrel load of cancer in my lungs, chest and neck. How is this possible? I didn't smoke. There is NO cancer in my family. There is no reason this would happen to me.

So I now have an oncologist. I didn't even know what an oncologist was. I was sat down after what felt like a million tests and told that I have a primary of lung cancer that has left the lungs so is in its final stages. It is incurable. If I am "lucky" I have 12 months to live. I admit I demanded to know this. I did not want anyone pretending. Am I going to die? Yes.

When someone tells you this, it is not something you can comprehend. It is so unbelievable that you just can't seem to find a place in your brain to put it. So I wanted to cry. I wanted to really wail. But I couldn't breathe well by this stage so couldn't. I couldn't even let the pain out. It was trapped inside me.

Andrew was a part of me at this time. I clung to him like I never had before. I needed him to save me. I begged him to save me and he promised me he would. I know he can't but I just couldn't accept this fate. We researched continuously. We had to know everything. We needed to know the odds of survival, every treatment we could use, and every new treatment coming out. Andrew abandoned work and plowed into the unknown. Fighting for my life.

My Life's Work

And my beautiful children. I need to tell you about each one individually as they are each my life's work.

Firstly, my one and only son Joshua. He's now 10. Some people age like a good wine. That is Joshua. He is someone I so want to see grow up as he changes everyday. He was such an energetic difficult young man, but everyday he seems to stumble into himself and is now discovering ambition and drive. I really am so intrigued as to where life will take him and who he will be. I want to see that it was all worthwhile. That all that hard work I have put into him will pay off into this glorious young man. I am convinced it will be so.

Jessica, 8 years old. She was born so quiet and has kept such a lovely placid nature. She is extremely intelligent, loving, watchful, thoughtful. Someone you can't not like. Everyone finds her adorable, you just can't help it. Such an easy child to raise. No problems at all.

Kristy, 4 years old. Wow, does this child have spunk. Never a boring moment and not in a bad way. She is fun with a capital "F." I have so enjoyed every second I have had with her. No pre-school for her as I couldn't bear to be apart from her for a second. She has been my best friend since she was born. I am obsessed by this little person. She fascinates me. She brings the whole family together. The link between us all.

These are my life's work. I have put 100% of myself into these people and sadly 0% into myself. How many mothers are guilty of that? Most of us I would think. Its hard work, but we don't want regrets with our children. We want to give them the best we can so that one day in the future we can look back and know we did the best we could. The very best. We can sit back and finally relax and know we have done it. Maybe they won't be perfect, but hopefully happy. That's all we really want for them. To be happy in whatever they decide to do.

So now I am told my children won't have a mother in 12 months. But I promised myself to raise these children. I got pregnant and thought it was a guarantee that I would be able to raise them. Not abandon them like this. No one told me this could happen. How can I promise to give them everything in life and then just not be there? I can't understand how this can happen. And I had to tell them this. How can you tell a child that their mother is going to die? How! But we did.

We were told to be honest with them. That if we weren't someone else might be, so better it came from us.

My beautiful Jessica and I had always planned a trip to the Bahamas when she turned 18. We talked about it a lot. This was funnily enough the first thing she said. "What about our trip to the Bahamas?" I wanted to say—"Oh right, yes OK, I will wait till after that to die," but couldn't. Our plans were shattered. The kids cried a lot. Josh sat on my knee and then his Dad's and Jess sat on Dad's knee then mine. We cuddled, we cried, we asked each other "Why?" but couldn't answer. Little Dolly (Kristy) cried but I don't think she really understood. It's hard to tell with a 4 year old. What a horrible night that was. A sunny day that rained and rained. We had no hope, but we had each other. . . .

> **FAST FACT**
>
> The five-year survival rate for people diagnosed with stage IV non-small cell lung cancer is 1 percent, according to the National Cancer Institute's Surveillance, Epidemiology, and End Results database.

Chemo

Chemo really drains you physically. It doesn't just make you sick and tired, but plays with your blood, and causes havoc in your body. With radiation as well, after the chemo infusion I always had this burning feeling through my chest. It was so intense at times I thought I wouldn't make it through the night. I remember one night, about 4 nights after the infusion Andrew went out to soccer with friends. I sat in the kitchen when he left and cried. I was in so much pain, but he left me alone with the kids anyway. I don't think he realised what was going on, or just needed to get out. But I thought I was going to die that night. When the kids were asleep I went up to each of them and said my goodbyes. I truly thought that was it. But I did survive the night and soon came to realise that pain like that was to become very common and something I had to deal with daily.

I soon hit a point when just breathing in and out was painful and I needed constant oxycontin tablets to help control it. Even with medication the pain never left. The pain became such that I could no longer lie on my side or my stomach. I could only lie on my back. I find this very hard to adjust to as I always lied on my belly, but since I was diagnosed I never have again. It's these little things that drive me mad.

I am not a vomiter. So when I get nauseous, I just feel extremely sick with no relief. To vomit would have helped. I was told to put weight on as I would be losing a lot of it while on chemotherapy. So when I can eat I should. I did this and I have never lost weight. I am now always bigger than I was at first. I was told something like 80% of cancer patients die of malnutrition. That certainly won't be me.

The day of the chemotherapy is not so bad. Andrew and I would sometimes even go out to lunch afterwards. I would feel fine with a normal appetite. By the next day and then for another 3–4 days the side effects hit. No appetite, nausea, the burning sensation through my chest, very tired and a bit scrabbled in the brain. Just felt like curling up in a ball and being left alone in a dark corner.

The good news is that within a couple of weeks I could feel the lumps in my neck decreasing in size. So it seemed that the treatment was working. At least for now. The combination of radiation and chemotherapy seemed to be doing the trick. After 3 weeks we did the first x-ray and it showed some changes. After the second cycle we did a

CT scan and things again seemed to be improving, especially the areas in my chest and neck. The lymph nodes seemed to be shrinking. I was always told the treatment was there to just help prolong my life a little. At least I had more than a few weeks.

Andrew and I had researched a lot by this point. More so Andrew as I was too busy being the sick cancer patient. Apparently 9 months was the average survival time of a lung cancer patient at my stage (IV). 9 months. I don't know why I want to know these statistics. We are all different and we never know how long we each have. Each patient responds differently to treatment. Through research we found what we thought would be our next treatment and sort out doctors that could provide it. We also used this time to get second opinions and after consulting a couple of Sydney [Australia] doctors and they all gave us the same diagnosis and recommended the same treatment we were confident we were doing the right thing. At least the treatment was appropriate for the time being. . . .

The Cancer Is Taking Over Again

It's June, 2007. I have been battling this cancer now for 17 months. That sounds like a long time, and I guess it certainly feels like it. I was given 12 months, so I guess its nice to have had an extra 5 months so far with my kids that I wasn't supposed to have. As time continues the chances of my "miracle" are diminishing before my eyes. The cancer is getting stronger and that is unfortunately the news of the day.

Last Friday I had a CT scan and today the results are in. Progression. How I hate that word. It means the cancer has spread. The cancer in my lungs has multiplied. I am getting worse, and the cancer is getting stronger and more resilient [resistant] to treatment.

Part of the report said I had a cancerous abdominal lymph node. When I questioned this I was told to ignore it, the bigger problem is your lungs. Ignore it? How do I ignore it? It may be only 14mm, but it is still new. Why does there come a point where it is so bad that new things don't matter? That is not right. This is happening more and more with my reports. For example my brain. When I last talked about all the new brain lesions I had I was told, don't worry, they are only small, just worry about your lungs. How can I ignore cancer in my brain? I can't. I worry about it all. I want it all to be treated and it all to go away. I want nothing less. I feel like the doctors are starting to give up on me. I really believe this is happening.

I also think everyone else is giving up on me too. I look sick now and am in constant pain so people look at me like I am dying. I see it in [their] eyes. They looked at me like that when I was first diagnosed and now it's back again.

Andrew talks positive but looks at me like hope is fading. He whispers to his friends and family on the phone as he doesn't want me to hear. He is getting grumpy at me. I think he is getting sick of taking care of me now. I am a big drain on him. I don't whinge [complain]. I try to be what he wants me to, positive and helpful. But I can't do much around here and he is getting sick of taking care of me. He looks at the future and can see me not in it. He can sometimes even discuss life without me in it. He would never do that before.

I watch the children and Andrew together and I hate it, but know they will make it without me. It is so sad my girls will have to grow up with no Mum, but they will. . . .

Unfair

It is so unfair. I want my time. I want now to be about me. I will never get my time. Never. I am now too sick to work and too sick to enjoy any benefits it would bring. I can't even walk. I can't even drive my kids to school. I am useless. My life is over. I will never get to experience what

I want. I want my future back. I want a chance to do and be what I dreamed of. All I have been so far is a mother. A great mother. But now I want some me time. I want to prove what I can do for me. I want so much and I need to be well to live it. I want to be well and live. Please, why is this something I can't have? Shouldn't everyone deserve this? I can't bear to lose my future. How do I cope with this? I really can't bear to see my life go up in smoke. It is so unfair!

So yes, at times I find it hard to breathe and not just literally. I can't handle the injustice of this cancer. It has ripped such a big part of me away that I really can't seem to breathe. And again I ask "Why Me?, What did I do that was so wrong that I deserve this?"

A Painful Death

Iraj Isaac Rahmim

In the following viewpoint writer Iraj Isaac Rahmim recounts the sorrowful death of his uncle Parviz. Rahmim describes the painful experience of watching his uncle die from lung cancer, which ultimately turned his skin yellow and scarred his nose and forehead. Rahmim believes through his writing—about both the death and the life of Parviz—that perhaps he can transform the pain from his uncle's loss into something more comfortable.

My Uncle Parviz died of lung cancer at 9:50 in the morning on a beautiful December day. . . . I wanted very much to sit outside away from the house, perhaps in a cafe, and pretend to be on vacation. . . .

The night before we knew the end was near. His breathing had become more labored, "from the head," as the hospice nurse had told us. Lying on the bed, unshaven with his nails grown long, his skin turning mustardy yellow, his nose and forehead scarred from the disease

SOURCE: Iraj Isaac Rahmim, "The Road from Kermanshah: How Parviz Came to Die," *Commonweal*, August 13, 2004. Reproduced by permission of Commonweal Foundation.

and falls, and with his arm and leg muscles melted away, he looked very much like my grandfather, his father, who had died ten months earlier—one day less. His breathing had an echoey hollow sound like the rapid blowing and releasing of a small balloon with great, and thankfully unconscious, effort. His bedroom had the stale smell of disease and decline.

My cousin David, the younger of Parviz's two sons, and I sat on the living room carpet, playing a mediocre yet aggressive game of chess, drinking freezer-kept vodka, and running to the darkened bedroom every time we thought we couldn't hear breathing over the unreliable baby monitor. My mother, having arrived all the way from Tehran on Sunday, for the second time in as many months, sat quietly on a chair listening to Louise, Parviz's wife. . . .

"Owning" the Dying Process

His breathing did deteriorate during the night, but in the morning I managed to convince Louise to go to work anyway. I felt this was the day, but what if he did last for another six weeks? She couldn't do much anyway. My mother staying home was trouble enough. I had already yelled at her once about interfering with our work. I had developed a sense of "ownership" of my uncle's dying process, as though we were partners in this. He would die, I would help and comfort, and be transformed. Perhaps this was my urgent attempt at repairing the strains in my relationship with Parviz that had developed as I grew older and asserted myself as an adult. I cannot say that we had less love for one another during the last few years, but less friendship, less intimacy. . . .

"His breathing is not good at all," my mother called out to me. . . . It was true. His mouth was slightly open, blocked by his soft and bloated tongue. I placed an eye-dropper of concentrated morphine under his tongue. "Parviz joon, this is Iraj. I am putting some painkiller under your tongue so you will be more comfortable. My mom is here also." She held his hand. They had told us that hearing is the last sense to go; perhaps he could hear me. Some of the morphine dribbled out from the corner of his mouth. Maybe some got absorbed, I thought.

His hearing was the last to go. Only the day before, when my mother sat beside his bed, sing-songing to him with her sad flowery Kermanshahi accent, "Did you see what happened to us, my little brother, my little beloved? May I die for you," he gathered up some strength, rolled his eyes toward her, no longer able even to tilt his head, and whispered, "God forbid." His typical sense of humor and verbal bantering had in fact lasted as late as Saturday, after the falls and the insertion of the bladder tube. That day, after that last humiliation, we had all gathered around him, sisters and wife, and children and niece and nephew, trying to convince him not to get off the bed, that he no longer needed to exert himself for the long walk to the bathroom, talking to him like a child with only half a mind. During a pause, he looked up severely, and with an angry-looking face said: "I want to go beteram." Seeing the confused look on all of our faces, he smiled and translated from Kurdish, which he spoke in addition to English and Persian, "you don't know what beteram means? It means I want to go fart," and quietly laughed at our expense, with his head down. . . .

When we first saw Parviz on Thursday night, I thought that he looked better than expected. He was asleep, unshaven, had lost some weight, looking older than his fifty-nine years. But he appeared nowhere close to death, or someone who has "two nights." Actually, the two nights had already expired. He really doesn't look too bad, I thought. Even on Friday morning, in the light of day, he wasn't doing too badly to my eye. He was awake, in bed, and cried when he saw us. . . .

He seemed cognizant of who we were, and what was going on. The crying was the proof. . . .

Improved Morale, Improved Health

Since the diagnosis in August, we had all become used to seeing Parviz cry. His low morale was a frequent topic of discussion. We were all united in thinking that improved morale would help him fight the disease and live longer. I, the acknowledged scientist of the family, quoted vague studies to this effect while others expressed surprise at his weakness. . . . I had decided that the solution was humor, and preached and practiced this often. His friends spent hours trying to cheer him up; consequently he had stopped taking most visitors. We all saw his low morale as moral weakness; he was surely not riding high into the sunset.

During Parviz's last few days, every time something went wrong, Louise would shake her head and mournfully say that even "this is a wedding party," meaning compared to what was to come next. One of the worst things about watching someone die is that there is nothing to look forward to. The patient is surely going to get worse, losing mental and physical functions gradually. As the body is slowly stripped of the soul, layer-by-layer, it becomes simply a mechanical collection of parts and resulting functions: eating, drinking, breathing, urinating, defecating. Painfully, even these are then taken, one by one, at which point there is nothing to declare but defeat. . . .

Our conversations "with" him that day would continue to center around medication, food, water, and his beloved overly sweetened iced tea. His answers, progressively more abbreviated, were reduced at times to up or down nods. He seemed to enjoy his iced tea and a small piece of cake that I fed him slowly, in place of a proper meal, which he could no longer swallow. I theorized, optimistically, that as long as there is joy, even of the minutest nature, life is worth living and preserving. This simple joy would not last long, of course, as on the next day, a tiny speck of sweet from his provincial birthplace of Kermanshah, just flown over eight thousand miles by my mother, would be his last food. . . .

The Reason for Writing

Why am I writing this story? Is it to put these memories on paper before I forget the exact sound of Parviz's voice, the feel of his meaty and powerfully large hands, and his humor? I have already begun to forget the look and sound of his laughter. Am I trying to close the book on the pain of watching him decline or to remind myself of what he meant to me when I was a child? So many of my fondest childhood memories involve him: when he came to Tehran on business and stayed with us, or when we went to Kermanshah for month-long summer holidays.

Like many in my family, Parviz was a great raconteur. His tales were joyful and juicy, and made you want to follow him around and do as he did. He had a wonderful provincial accent, with all the "wrong" vowels and unexpected extra consonants, which made the simplest word mysterious to my ears and his tales fun to hear for even the tenth time. I remember a story from his army days when a friend took him for lunch to his father's village estate, and the father, a Khan, ordered a feast by his river under the trees which included a whole sheep grilled, and they cut chunks of meat with large knives right from the fire, and ate just like that with their hands, "with a lot of salt, a lot of pepper."

Once every few months Parviz came to Tehran to buy parts, and he stayed with us. I remember these visits vividly. On his time off, he and I would go to the movies or have lunch, and sometimes I tagged along and went to the southern parts of the city, where the bazaar and all the merchants were, normally off-limits to me, and watched him bargain and buy. Some days he would volunteer to cook for us the only dish he seemed to know, "something that will make you want to eat your fingers." It was an amalgam of eggplant, tomato, chicken, salt and pepper eaten with lots of bread—the kind of dish you imagine men learn to make as bachelors or when in the army.

I have noticed, happily, that after writing about painful experiences, the act of writing itself becomes incorporated into the original story. The unpleasant childhood memory of my parents' fight becomes the pleasurable memory of a narrative well written, losing the old hold on my mind. Perhaps with writing about Parviz, not only his death but also his life, I am attempting to transform the pain of his loss into something better, something comfortable. Could it be that death, then, really is not closing the book after all?

Reflecting on those—my uncle's—last few days, I find myself more at peace with the idea of death. Having observed, or rather participated in, the process once, it is no longer an unknown to fear. The decline may take long, and may well be painful, uncomfortable, and even lonely, but at least I have seen it and know what to expect. . . .

A couple of days before dying, Parviz's urine bag came open as we tried to re-adjust him, and poured urine down my knee and leg. I laughed. There is a story about my first trip as a baby to Kermanshah. My mother had just cleaned me and before putting a fresh diaper on, brought me out naked to show to my aunt and uncle who were in bed. As she held me up by my underarms in front of them, it appears I decided that further release was in order, right on my aunt and uncle. All three adults present always tell the rest of the story accompanied with wild flailing arm motions and gargling drowning sounds, and laughter. Now, feeling

> **FAST FACT**
>
> Every thirty seconds, someone, somewhere in the world, dies of lung cancer, according to the Global Lung Cancer Coalition.

the warm dark yellow-and-rust-color urine on my leg, I also laughed. I had urinated on Parviz early in my life, and in his own humorous fashion, he had paid me back at the end of his.

Early on the afternoon of that Tuesday, the two men slowly rolled Parviz's tightly wrapped body, with the outline of his hands placed on his chest visible, out through the garage and into one of the vans. Passing through the darkened garage, seeing us all standing around, one facing the gurney, another Parviz's wood working bench and tools, yet a third looking at his beloved Chevy Blazer, as always meticulously clean, and another facing the empty wall looking at nothing at all, one of the men paused for a moment, looked down, and said gently: "Please don't worry. We'll take good care of him."

The Sorrow of Death

The next morning, I sat at one of two limping outdoor metal tables at a coffee-and-bagel shop, shifting my tailbone from side to side on the narrow uncomfortable chair, a sagging paper cup in hand. . . . In reality, it was a beautiful Wednesday. . . . But I couldn't really sense the beauty, sitting there, alone, staring at the old car and the pebbles and bits of bagel and bread on the ground. . . .

What remains of a man, dead?

Sensations remain, of the feel of the skin, its roughness and temperature, in a handshake or an embrace, of the inflection of the voice or the cracking of laughter, of the childhood joy of a surprise visitor from a far-off town. Objects remain. Photographs, handicrafts, a favorite chair, or a zucchini patch planted years ago. There will be memories of events and of stories told. We will repeat these memories until they are ingrained into our children's consciousness, even as they are diluted with every retelling, like genes passed through generations. With time, objects are recalled less intensely, sensations fade, and favorite tales take up a different voice, the new voice of the living, and no longer that of the loved one lost. But perhaps also in time, these memories simply embed themselves so deeply into our minds and our flesh that we no longer notice them as external. They become one with us and our children, integrated and comfortable. And so we might be excused for believing that the loved one remains with us after all.

But at first, there is sorrow.

GLOSSARY

adenocarcinoma	Cancer arising from the glandular cells or epithelial tissues. Adenocarcinoma of the lung is a type of non-small cell lung cancer and the most common form of lung cancer in the United States.
alveoli	Tiny air sacs at the end of the bronchioles in the lungs.
angiogenesis	Tumor angiogenesis is the growth of new blood vessels that tumors need to grow. This is caused by the release of chemicals by the tumor.
asbestos	A natural material that is made of tiny threads or fibers and was used to insulate homes. The fibers can enter the lungs as a person breathes and cause many diseases, including lung cancer.
aspiration	Removal of fluid from a lump, often a cyst, with a needle and a syringe.
biopsy	To remove cells or tissue from the body for testing and examination under a microscope.
bronchi	The large airways connecting the windpipe to the lungs. The singular form is *bronchus*.
bronchioles	The smaller air passages leading from the bronchi into the lobes of the lung.
bronchitis	Inflammation and swelling of the bronchi.
bronchoscopy	A way to look at the inside of the windpipe, the bronchi, and/or the lungs using a lighted tube inserted through the patient's nose or mouth.
cancer	Diseases in which abnormal cells divide without control. Cancer cells can invade nearby tissues and can spread through the bloodstream and lymphatic system (bone marrow, spleen, thymus, and lymph nodes) to other parts of the body.

carcinogen	A cancer-causing agent.
carcinoma	Cancer arising from the epithelial cells that cover or line internal and external body surfaces.
chemotherapy	Treatment that involves administering medicines that kill cancer cells. Chemotherapy is a systemic treatment, which means it flows through the bloodstream and reaches every part of the body.
clinical trial	A kind of research study where patients volunteer to test new ways of screening for, preventing, finding, or treating a disease.
computed or computerized tomography (CT) scan	A set of detailed pictures of areas inside the body, taken from different angles. The pictures are made by a computer linked to an X-ray machine.
emphysema	A disease that affects the tiny air sacs in the lungs. Emphysema makes it harder to breathe. People who smoke have a greater chance of getting emphysema.
epidermal growth factor (EGF)	A protein in the body that stimulates some cells, including some cancer cells, to grow and multiply.
epidermal growth factor receptor (EGFR)	A receptor on the surface of cells that binds to the epidermal growth factor protein.
epidermal growth factor receptor (EGFR) inhibitor	A class of anticancer drugs that work by blocking epidermal growth factor from stimulating cells to grow.
epithelial cells	Cells that make up the epithelial tissues that cover the outside of the body (skin) and that also cover and line the insides and outsides of organs. Cancer of the epithelial cells (called carcinomas) are the most common form of cancer. Different types of epithelial cells include squamous cells and glandular cells.
epithelial tissue	Tissue that covers and lines the body. As well as covering the outside of the body, epithelial cells cover the inside, too.
esophagus	The tube that carries food from the throat to the stomach.

first-line therapy	The first course of treatment used against a disease.
five-year survival rate	The number of patients who are alive five years after a diagnosis of cancer.
large cell carcinoma	Non-small cell lung cancers that cannot be classified as squamous cell carcinomas or adenocarcinomas.
lobe	A part of an organ, such as the lung.
lobectomy	Surgery to remove a lobe of an organ.
lymph nodes	Small glands that form the immune system to help the body fight infection and disease. They filter a fluid called lymph and contain white blood cells.
lymphoma	Cancer that begins in the lymphatic cells of the immune system.
magnetic resonance imaging (MRI)	A type of body scan that uses a magnet linked to a computer to make detailed pictures of areas inside the body. An MRI can be used to find cancer.
mediastinum	The mass of tissues and organs separating the two lungs. Includes the heart and its large vessels, the trachea, esophagus, thymus, lymph nodes, and other structures and tissues.
metastasis	The spread of cancer from one part of the body (primary growth) to another.
non-small cell lung cancer (NSCLC)	The most common form of lung cancer. The cells of NSCLC are larger than those of small cell lung cancer. There are several different types of NSCLC; the three most common types are squamous cell carcinoma, adenocarcinoma, and large cell carcinoma.
oncologist	A doctor who specializes in studying and treating cancer.
oncology	The branch of medicine concerned with the study, diagnosis, treatment, and prevention of cancer.
pleura	The thin lining that covers the lungs and the inside of the chest wall that cushions the lungs.

pneumonectomy	The removal of an entire lung.
positron emission tomography (PET) scan	A scan that uses a cancer's rapidly dividing cells to make a diagnosis. Radiologists give the patient a radioactive sugar substance that will be absorbed more by the cancer than by normal tissues, due to the cancer cells' increased need for energy. The PET scan records the areas where the radioactivity is focused.
radiation therapy	The use of high-energy radiation from X-rays, neutrons, and other sources to kill cancer cells and shrink tumors. Radiation therapy affects cancer cells in a targeted area.
radon	An odorless, colorless gas known to increase the risk of cancer. Radon comes from rocks and dirt and can get trapped in houses and buildings.
small cell lung cancer (SCLC)	A type of lung cancer made up of small, round cells. SCLC is less common than non-small cell lung cancer and often grows more quickly.
sputum	The substance expelled from the lungs that contains mucus, cellular debris, microorganisms, blood, and/or pus.
sputum cytology	A screening test for lung cancer where sputum coughed up from the lungs is examined under a microscope to check for abnormal or cancerous cells.
squamous cell	A type of epithelial cell found in the skin, the lining of the hollow organs (such as the lungs), and in the breathing and digestive tracts.
squamous cell carcinoma	A type of cancer that begins in the squamous cells.
stage	The stage of a cancer is a descriptor (usually numbers I to IV) of how much the cancer has spread. Staging is typically based on the size of the primary tumor and the presence or absence of lymphatic involvement or metastases.
targeted therapies	Drugs that are specifically designed to interfere with the functioning or formation of cancer cells. These drugs can block

specific substances involved in cancer cell growth, or they can cause cancer cells to die.

thoracic surgeon A doctor who specializes in chest, heart, and lung surgery.

trachea The airway connecting the larynx to the lungs; windpipe.

tumor An abnormal mass of tissue that results from excessive cell division. Tumors perform no useful body function and may be either benign (not cancerous) or malignant (cancerous).

CHRONOLOGY

B.C. **2500–1600**   Egyptian writings contain descriptions of cancer.

B.C. **460–370**   Hippocrates gives the name *karkinos* and *karkinoma* (from the Greek for "crab") to a group of diseases, including cancers of the breast, uterus, stomach, and skin.

A.D. **130–200**   Roman physician Galen uses the word *oncos* (Greek for "swelling") to describe tumors. Although Galen removes some tumors surgically, he generally believes that cancer is best left untreated.

1110–1500   Cancer is thought to arise from an excess of black bile.

1500–1590   Ambroise Paré—the era's best-known surgeon—recommends surgery for cancer only if tumors can be totally removed.

1600–1670   Lymph abnormalities begin to be examined as possible cancer causes.

1700   French physician Claude Deshais Gendron publishes *Enquiries into the Nature, Knowledge, and Cure of Cancers,* in which he concludes that cancer arises locally in the body as a hard, growing mass. He believes that it is untreatable with drugs and that tumors should be removed surgically.

1700   Italian physician Bernardino Ramazzini publishes *De Morbis Artificum Diatriba,* Latin for *Discourse on the Diseases of Workers,* in which he says that certain diseases are correlated with specific exposures, including heavy metals and dust, with cancer in miners and industrial workers.

1758   Henri F. LeDran describes operations on several cases of cancer in a manual prepared for students, *Observations in Surgery Containing One Hundred and Fifteen Different Cases with Particular Remarks on Each, for the Improvement of Young Adults.*

1761   Italian pathologist Giovanni Morgagni publishes a thorough written description of cancer.

1878   Malignant lung tumors represent 1 percent of all cancers seen at autopsy in the Institute of Pathology of the University of Dresden in Germany.

1880   Virginian James Albert Bonsack invents the first cigarette rolling machine.

1895   German physicist Wilhelm Roentgen discovers X-rays.

1896   Emil Grubbe, a Chicago medical student, uses X-rays to treat a cancer patient.

1913   The American Society for the Control of Cancer is established (later to become the American Cancer Society).

1918   Malignant lung tumors represent 10 percent of all cancers seen at autopsy in the Institute of Pathology of the University of Dresden in Germany.

1926–1932   Lung cancer in miners (due to radon gas) in Germany and Czechoslovakia is recognized as an occupational disease—and the miners are entitled to compensation.

1929   German physician Fritz Lickint publishes a paper showing that lung cancer patients are particularly likely to be smokers.

1930   The *Springer Handbook of Special Pathology* notes that malignant lung tumors began to increase at the turn of the century and may still be increasing. Smoking is briefly mentioned as a possibility, but it is discounted due to lack of evidence.

1933   American physician Evarts A. Graham performs the first successful pneumonectomy on a lung cancer patient at Barnes Hospital in St. Louis, Missouri.

1933–1945   The German Nazis undertake a massive antismoking campaign.

1937   Congress passes the National Cancer Institute Act and authorizes annual funding for cancer research.

1939   The National Cancer Institute is formed through the merger of the Office of Cancer Investigations at Harvard University and a pharmacology division at the National Institutes of Health.

1939–1940   German Franz H. Müller publishes a case-control study regarding the connection between tobacco use and lung cancer. Müller states that the rising incidence of lung cancer is directly linked to the rise in tobacco use.

1943 German scientists Eberhard Schairer and Erich Schö-niger, working at the German Institute for Tobacco Hazards, find that among 109 lung cancer cases, only 3 are in nonsmokers.

1946 Two pharmacologists, Louis S. Goodman and Alfred Gilman, working for the U.S. Department of Defense in collaboration with thoracic surgeon Gustav Linskog, realize that cancer tumors can be treated by pharmacological agents. The scientists inject mustine (related to mustard gas) into a patient with non-Hodgkin's lymphoma in one of the first uses of chemotherapy.

1950 British epidemiologists Richard Doll and Austin Bradford Hill begin the long-running "British doctors study," which provides statistical proof that smoking tobacco increases the risk of lung cancer.

Early 1950s Lung cancer surpasses colon cancer as the number one cancer killer in men.

1955 Congress funds a National Chemotherapy Program to test compounds that might be effective against cancer.

1961 Judah Folkman of Harvard University discovers that tumors create a network of blood vessels to bring them oxygen so they can grow. He calls this process angiogenesis.

1964 Surgeon general Luther L. Terry releases a report of the Surgeon General's Advisory Committee on Smoking and Health, which concludes that cigarette smoking is a cause of lung cancer and laryngeal cancer in men and a probable cause of lung cancer in women.

1965 Congress passes the Federal Cigarette Labeling and Advertising Act requiring the surgeon general's warnings on all cigarette packages.

1969 This year's edition of the *Springer Handbook of Special Pathology* uses twenty-five pages to discuss the role of cigarette smoking in causing lung cancer.

1975 Minnesota becomes the first state to ban smoking in most public spaces.

Late 1980s Lung cancer surpasses breast cancer as the number one cancer killer in women.

1990 The federal government bans smoking on all interstate buses and all domestic airline flights lasting six hours or less.

1990s For the first time, lung cancer death rates begin decreasing in men.

1996 Larry Clark finds that selenium reduces the risk of lung, colon, and prostate cancer.

2001 The surgeon general issues *Women and Smoking*, a report detailing the health impact of smoking on females.

ORGANIZATIONS TO CONTACT

The editors have compiled the following list of organizations concerned with the issues debated in this book. The descriptions are derived from materials provided by the organizations. All have publications or information available for interested readers. The list was compiled on the date of publication of the present volume; the information provided here may change. Be aware that many organizations take several weeks or longer to respond to inquiries, so allow as much time as possible.

American Association for Cancer Research (AACR)
615 Chestnut St.
17th Fl.
Philadelphia, PA
19106-4404
(215) 440-9300 or
(866) 423-3965
fax: (215) 440-9313
www.aacr.org

The AACR is one of the oldest professional associations devoted to cancer research. Its mission is to prevent and cure cancer through research, education, communication, and collaboration. Through its programs and services, the AACR fosters research in cancer and related biomedical science; accelerates the dissemination of new research findings among scientists and others dedicated to the conquest of cancer; promotes science education and training; and advances the understanding of cancer etiology, prevention, diagnosis, and treatment throughout the world. The AACR is the scientific partner of Stand Up to Cancer, a collaboration of the entertainment industry. The AACR publishes *CR* magazine.

American Cancer Society (ACS)
1599 Clifton Rd. NE
Atlanta, GA 30329
(800) 227 2345
fax: (404) 329-5787
www.cancer.org

The ACS is a nationwide, community-based, voluntary health organization dedicated to eliminating cancer as a major health problem by preventing cancer, saving lives, and diminishing suffering from cancer through research, education, advocacy, and service. The ACS publishes three peer-reviewed scientific periodicals: *CA: A Cancer Journal for Clinicians; Cancer;* and *Cancer Cytopathology.*

American Lung Association (ALA)
1301 Pennsylvania Ave. NW
Washington, DC 20004
(202) 785-3355
fax: (202) 452-1805
www.lungusa.org

The ALA is a national nonprofit organization that works to save lives by improving lung health and preventing lung disease through education, advocacy, and research. The organization focuses on trying to prevent teen smoking and on advocating for antismoking and air protection laws. The ALA publishes an e-newsletter and several annual reports such as the *State of the Air*, the *State of Tobacco Control*, *Lung Disease Data*, and others.

American Society of Clinical Oncology (ASCO)
2318 Mill Rd., Ste. 800
Alexandria, VA 22314
(888) 282-2552 or
(571) 483-1300
www.asco.org

ASCO is a nonprofit organization composed of oncologists with the overarching goals of improving cancer care and prevention. The ASCO Cancer Foundation was established by ASCO as its philanthropic arm to fund research and education programs both in the United States and abroad. The society also provides oncologist-approved cancer information on the Web site www.cancer.net. Additionally, ASCO publishes the *Journal of Clinical Oncology* and the *Journal of Oncology Practice*.

The Beverly Fund
PO Box 330266
San Francisco, CA 94133-0266
(415) 894-2470
www.beverlyfund.org

The Beverly Fund is a national nonprofit organization dedicated to lung cancer awareness, patient support, early detection, and research. The Beverly Fund's mission is to put a face on lung cancer and to give a voice to those who have been affected by lung cancer. The organization provides fact sheets and the *Lung Source Newsletter*.

Lung Cancer Alliance
888 Sixteenth St. NW Ste. 150
Washington, DC 20006
(202) 463-2080 or
(800) 298-2436
www.lungcancer alliance.org

The Lung Cancer Alliance is dedicated solely to advocating for people living with lung cancer or those at risk for the disease. Its initiatives aim to educate public policy leaders of the need for greater resources for lung cancer research while changing the face of lung cancer and reducing the stigma associated with the disease. It also offers patient education and support programs focused on helping people directly affected by lung cancer. The organization offers fact sheets, patient support materials, and two newsletters: *New Directions* and *Lung Cancer Alliance Times*.

Lung Cancer Foundation of America
15 S. Franklin St.
New Ulm, MN 56073
(507) 354-1361
www.lcfamerica.org

The Lung Cancer Foundation of America's mission is to save lives by improving the survival rate of lung cancer by raising money from the private sector and channeling those funds to lung cancer researchers so that researchers find effective ways to predict, detect, and treat lung cancer. The foundation's Web site provides blogs such as *Lung Cancer . . . Through My Eyes* and *Inhaling Life, Exhaling Our Experiences.*

Lung Cancer Research Foundation
845 Third Ave., 6th Fl.
New York, NY 10022
(646) 290-5154
fax: (646) 290-5001
www.lungcancerre
searchfoundation.org

The mission of the Lung Cancer Research Foundation is to support national research studies and activities focused on developing innovative strategies for better treatments, screening, and prevention of all cancers of the lung. The foundation sponsors annual Strides for Life to raise money for lung cancer research. It also hosts lunches and seminars and publishes the newsletter *Pathways.*

National Cancer Institute (NCI)
NCI Public Inquiries Office
6116 Executive Blvd.
Rm. 3036A
Bethesda, MD 20892-8322
(800) 422-6237
www.cancer.gov

The NCI is one of the twenty-seven institutes and centers that make up the National Institutes of Health. The institute coordinates the National Cancer Program, which conducts and supports research, training, health information dissemination, and other programs with respect to the cause, diagnosis, prevention, and treatment of cancer. The NCI conducts research in its own laboratories and clinics and collaborates with volunteer organizations and other national and foreign institutions engaged in cancer research and training activities. The institute publishes a biweekly newsletter, the *NCI Cancer Bulletin.*

National Lung Cancer Partnership (NLCP)
222 N. Midvale Blvd.
Ste. 6
Madison, WI 53705
(608) 233-7905
fax: (608) 233-7893
www.nationallungcan
cerpartnership.org

The NLCP is a nonprofit organization the mission of decreasing deaths due to lung cancer and helping patients live longer and better through research, awareness, and advocacy. The NLCP raises awareness of the deadly impact of lung cancer on both women and men; increases funding for lung cancer research; and improves patient care by educating and empowering patients and health-care professionals. The NLCP publishes *Living with a Diagnosis of Lung Cancer,* an educational booklet for newly diagnosed lung cancer patients, and the *Lung Cancer Voice,* a print newsletter, as well as an online blog called *Ask the Expert.*

FOR FURTHER READING

Books

David Alberts and Lisa Hess, *Fundamentals of Cancer Prevention*. New York: Springer, 2005.

American Cancer Society, *QuickFacts Lung Cancer: What You Need to Know—Now*. Atlanta: American Cancer Society, 2007.

Jim Beaver, *Life's That Way: A Memoir*. New York: Amy Einhorn, 2009.

Kate Darnton, Kayce Freed Jennings, and Lynn Sherr, *Peter Jennings: A Reporter's Life*. New York: PublicAffairs, 2007.

Joan Esherick, *Clearing the Haze: A Teen's Guide to Smoking-Related Health Issues*. Broomall, PA: Mason Crest, 2005.

Brian Fies, *Mom's Cancer*. New York: Abrams Image, 2006.

Patricia Ganz, *Cancer Survivorship: Today and Tomorrow*. New York: Springer, 2007.

Peter Gluckman and Mark Hanson, *Developmental Origins of Health and Disease*. Cambridge, UK: Cambridge University Press, 2006.

Claudia Henschke, *Lung Cancer: Myths, Facts, Choices—and Hope*. New York: Norton, 2003.

John Mendelsohn, *The Molecular Basis of Cancer*. Philadelphia: Saunders/Elsevier, 2008.

Suzanne Miller, *Individuals, Families, and the New Era of Genetics: Biopsychosocial Perspectives*. New York: Norton, 2006.

Joseph Panno, *Cancer: The Role of Genes, Lifestyle, and Environment*. New York: Facts On File, 2005.

J.H. Schiller, Karen Parles, and Amy Cipau, *100 Questions & Answers About Lung Cancer*. Sudbury, MA: Jones and Bartlett, 2010.

Sean Swarner, *Keep Climbing*. New York: Atria, 2007.

U.S. Surgeon General, *The Health Consequences of Involuntary Exposure to Tobacco Smoke: A Report of the Surgeon General.* Rockville, MD: U.S. Department of Health and Human Services, 2006.

Julie Walker, *Lung Cancer: Current and Emerging Trends in Detection and Treatment.* New York: Rosen, 2006.

Periodicals and Internet Sources

Todd Ackerman, "Promise in the Battle Against a Top Killer," *Houston Chronicle*, April 18, 2010.

Cancer Weekly, "Gene Is Linked to Lung Cancer Development in Never Smokers," April 6, 2010.

Geoffrey Cowley and Claudia Kalb, "The Deadliest Cancer," *Newsweek*, August 22, 2005.

CQ HealthBeat, "Blacks Smoke Less but More Likely to Contract Lung Cancer than Whites," April 12, 2010.

Emma Dorey, "Skin and Lung Cancer Decoded," *Chemistry and Industry*, January 11, 2010.

Economist, "A Strand Apart: Cancer and Stem Cells," January 16, 2010.

Linda Geddes, "Living with the Enemy," *New Scientist*, October 25, 2008.

Guelph (ON) Mercury, "My Dad's Smoking . . . and Me, I'm Burning," November 28, 2009.

Hamilton (ON) Spectator, "Test Predicts Smokers' Lethal Lung Cancer," April 8, 2010.

Weidong Han, Yali Zhao, and Xiaobing Fu, "Induced Pluripotent Stem Cells: The Dragon Awakens," *BioScience*, April 2010.

Harvard Review of Health News, "Green Tea May Affect Lung Cancer Risk," January 13, 2010.

Katherine Hobson, "How to Get the Very Best Cancer Care," *U.S. News & World Report*, November 30, 2009.

Charlotte Huff, "Lung Overdue," *Cure*, Spring 2010.

Judi Ketteler, "Lung Cancer Report," *Self*, October 2009.

Stephen Little, "Cancer Biomarkers—a Good Start," *Medical Laboratory Observer*, May 2009.

Lorraine V. Murray, "Don't Question Loved One's Illness," *Atlanta Journal-Constitution*, July 25, 2009.

New York Times, "Health: Lung Cancer," http://health.nytimes.com/health/guides/disease/lung-cancer/overview.html.

Craig Peacock and D. Neil Watkins, "Cancer Stem Cells and the Ontogeny of Lung Cancer," *Journal of Clinical Oncology*, June 10, 2008.

Janet Raloff, "Germs in Tobacco Potential Source for Infections Blamed on Smoking," *Science News*, March 13, 2010.

ScienceDaily, "Lung Cancer News," www.sciencedaily.com/news/health_medicine/lung_cancer.

Jill Smolowe, "Dana Reeve Brave to the End," *People Weekly*, March 27, 2006.

Nikhi Swaminathan, "Why Some Smokers Get Lung Cancer—and Others Are Spared," *Scientific American*, April 4, 2008.

Liz Szabo, "Look Closer at CT Scan Risks," *USA Today*, December 21, 2009.

Carly Weeks, "Study Explores Cancer, Stress Link," *Toronto Globe & Mail*, October 1, 2009.

Women's Health Weekly, "Hormone Replacement Therapy Linked to Increased Lung Cancer Risk," March 18, 2010.

INDEX